D0810655

THE SEA

edited and with an introduction by
WAYNE GRADY

THE SEA

A LITERARY COMPANION

 David Suzuki Foundation

 GREYSTONE BOOKS

D&M PUBLISHERS INC.

Vancouver/Toronto/Berkeley

Greystone Books
D&M Publishers Inc.
2323 Quebec Street, Suite 201
Vancouver BC, Canada V5T 4S7
www.greystonebooks.com

David Suzuki Foundation
219–2211 West 4th Avenue,
Vancouver BC, Canada V6K 4S2

Library and Archives Canada Cataloguing in Publication
The sea : a literary companion / edited by Wayne Grady.

ISBN 978-1-55365-395-0

1. Ocean—Literary collections. 2. Seas—Literary collections.
3. Sea stories. I. Grady, Wayne

PN6071.S4S42 2009   820.8'032162   C2008-908144-7

Jacket and text design by Peter Cocking
Typeset by Naomi MacDougall
Jacket image: Mary Evans Picture Library; background image: ©Bettmann/CORBIS
Printed and bound in Canada by Friesens
Printed on acid-free paper that is forest friendly (100% post-consumer recycled paper)
and has been processed chlorine free.
Distributed in the U.S. by Publishers Group West

We gratefully acknowledge the financial support of the Canada Council for the Arts,
the British Columbia Arts Council, the Province of British Columbia through the
Book Publishing Tax Credit, and the Government of Canada through the Book Publishing
Industry Development Program (BPIDP) for our publishing activities.

CONTENTS

INTRODUCTION

"WE ALL COME from the sea," John F. Kennedy once observed. "In our veins is the exact percentage of salt in our blood as exists in the ocean . . .When we go back to the sea, we are going back whence we came."

Kennedy's words ring true in several ways. Most scientists today agree that when life originated on this planet three and a half billion years ago, it originated at the bottom of the ocean, probably somewhere along the forty thousand-mile-long mid-ocean ridge that encircles the globe ten thousand feet below the oceans' surface like the seam of a very large baseball. Along the ridge, ruptures in the earth's lithospheric plates emit hot gasses, forming mineral clouds called "black smokers" that heat the surrounding water to more than seven hundred degrees Fahrenheit. Strange creatures cluster around these black smokers: pale, eyeless shrimp; six-foot-long, mouthless tubeworms; animals that breathe hydrogen sulfide instead of oxygen, can withstand temperatures that would parboil less-hardy organisms, and have entered into a symbiotic relationship with bacteria in order to process water molecules into food. Our best guess is that this deep-sea faunal assemblage sprang from the same multicelled life forms that we did.

There is also evidence of more recent connections to the sea. In the 1960s, Oxford marine biologist Sir Alister Hardy suggested that one of the direct ancestors of *Homo sapiens* was a semiaquatic hominid, an apelike mammal specially adapted to spend at least part of its life in the water. These were shore-dwelling proto-humans, rather than creatures of the savannahs. They lived primarily on shellfish, became excellent swimmers, and developed layers of subcutaneous, blubber-like fat to keep them warm and buoyant. Like dolphins, whales, seals, and otters, Hardy hypothesized, "perhaps Man had been aquatic, too."

In 1982, Hardy's theory was picked up by Elaine Morgan in her controversial book *The Aquatic Ape*. Morgan looked at modern humans and asked why we differ in certain suggestive ways from other African apes. Why are we the only hairless hominids? Hairlessness is an attribute of aquatic animals, not land-dwelling mammals. Why are we the only mammals with conscious breathing? All other terrestrial mammals breathe involuntarily, unable to hold their breath. The placement of the muscles in our throats allows us to open our mouths underwater without drowning. Even bipedalism is unique to humans; apes do not walk truly upright but, like most birds, keep their spinal columns nearly parallel to the ground. The only other truly bipedal animal is the penguin, which is also semi-aquatic.

Morgan suggested that this sea-dwelling ancestor lived beside the Danakil Strait, at the southern end of the Red Sea, about five million years ago, before the Asian landmass drifted over to connect with the African continent. After that cataclysmic contact, Morgan posited, our forebears retreated inland up the Rift Valley, where they evolved into a grassland species: perhaps the waving grass reminded them of the sea. Support for this contentious theory came in 1997, when two Italian paleontologists discovered the fossilized skeleton of *Oreopithecus bambolii* on the island of Sardinia. Now known as the "swamp ape," it seems to have been semi-aquatic, was bipedal in the modern sense, and was probably a lot fatter than we are. And in 2007, evidence of behaviorally modern humans dating back 164,000 years—70,000 years earlier than *Homo sapiens* was thought to have appeared—was found on the shore of the Indian Ocean, on the east coast of South Africa. Human beings have been gazing out over the sea for virtually all of our evolutionary history.

This may explain, in part, why sixty percent of the world's population lives in coastal areas and sixty-five percent of the world's largest cities are beside an ocean. Yes, seaside ports are convenient for shipping, but our affinity for the sea may have as much to do with nostalgia as with commerce. Perhaps it's no coincidence that virtually every culture on the planet has a flood myth. And, as the biographies of many of the writers in this collection attest, as individuals we are subject to otherwise inexplicable longings to go to sea. Charles Darwin, Herman Melville, Joshua Slocum, and Jack London all came to a moment in their lives when they were prepared to drop everything and join a

ship that was sailing for somewhere. Dora Birtles suddenly
decided to leave her husband and family in Australia, and with
four companions, none of whom were sailors, set out to circum-
navigate the world in a thirty-four-foot sailboat. Many of our
most popular adventure stories, from the novels of Jules Verne
and Patrick O'Brian to accounts of Arctic exploration and perfect storms, are sea stories. One of the most widely read books
in Elizabethan England was *Hakluyt's Voyages,* which gathered
together accounts of expeditions by sea to foreign lands, the
more arduous the better. In his book-length essay *Shipwreck,*
excerpted here, novelist John Fowles speculates on the strange
fascination we have for disasters at sea: "We derive from the
spectacle of calamity a sense of personal survival," he writes.
But perhaps it is also a sense of species survival; we know what
the sea can do because we used to live there.

One measure of how closely we are tied to the sea is to recall
how much of our language is related to it. In English, we no
longer speak much of fathoms (six feet) or leagues (three miles),
and we may have forgotten the seafaring origins of such phrases
as "the devil to pay" and "to let the cat out of the bag," but these
colorful idioms are not entirely metaphoric. The "devil" was
the widest part of the hull of a British merchant vessel, and "to
pay" meant to caulk with tar: paying the devil was the most dangerous job on a ship. And the cat, of course, was the cat-o'-nine-
tails, or the lash, which was kept in a leather bag when not in use.
Jonathan Raban, in his excerpt from *Passage to Juneau,* reminds
us of a few more common expressions of nautical origin; "the

bitter end," "taken aback," "aloof," and "by and large" are but a small sampling that emphasize the maritime roots of landlubber ways. Whenever we tell stories, we evoke the sea.

The sea's lure is undeniable and irresistible. In his poem "Sea Fever," John Masefield writes of the sea's eternal attraction:

> I must go down to the seas again, for the call of the running tide
> Is a wild call and a clear call that may not be denied . . .

I have spent many a mesmerized hour standing at a ship's rail listening to that wild, clear call, carried over three oceans, trying to account for its magnetic pull. No matter how tempestuous the sea, it is somehow satisfying to watch, as though a willful sea is the final confirmation of a natural power we have always suspected to be there and have always welcomed. It is a kind of relief. "Man marks the earth with ruin," Byron wrote in *Childe Harold's Pilgrimage*, but "his control / Stops with the shore." There is a fierce inevitability about the sea, "a pleasing fear," in Byron's phrase, wonderfully captured in E.J. Pratt's poem *The Titanic*. His description, included in this volume, of the iceberg fated to rendezvous with the "unsinkable" vessel has a chilling rightness to it. It is not indifferent Nature, it is Nature with a vengeance. It is justice we are watching.

Both John F. Kennedy and Sir Alister Hardy spoke of going *back* to the sea, and so we do; every year, sixty million more of us move from inland to the seashore. Many of us don't stop there. Although there are no statistics on the matter, I would wager that the ashes from a large proportion of human cremations are scattered over water rather than buried in the earth. Not surprisingly, an industry has sprung up to accommodate such requests. For $2,500, anyone can have their loved one's ashes mixed with marine-grade concrete, formed into a "reef ball"— a hollow, cone-shaped structure with softball-sized holes in the outer shell—and added to one of many "Eternal Reefs" built on a foundation of decommissioned army tanks off the eastern seaboard of North America. Marine organisms build upon the concrete balls, and very soon a natural undersea colony is formed. This, of course, gives a fresh pitch to Shakespeare's famous lines:

> Full fathom five thy father lies,
> Of his bones are coral made.

Coral, one of the oldest life-forms on Earth, is not far removed from those mystifying creatures still found around black smokers and so, like Sir Francis Drake and Joshua Slocum, we come full circle. The sea, both ever-changing and eternal, unquiet and peaceful, is a torment to the brain and a salve to the spirit. In these twenty-three selections, each of which evoke the beauty and the terror of the sea, we find the clues to both our origin and our destiny.

Wayne Grady

THE FLOOD

GENESIS 7: 1-24

That a great flood occurred during prerecorded history is a myth common to so many cultures it is difficult to ascribe the story to invention. In Greek mythology, Deucalion, son of Prometheus, and his wife were saved from a flood by floating in a large chest, eventually landing on Mount Parnassus; the Scandinavian giant Bergelmir survived a flood caused by the slaying of the ice-giant Ymir, whose blood formed the oceans; in Sumerian legend, the god Enlil warned the priest Ziusudra to build a great ship and to fill it with beasts and birds. Similar flood stories are found in African, North American, and South Sea island mythologies. The Christian and Judaic account, excerpted here, has thematic links to Islamic and East African versions (in Masai legend, Tumbainot sends a vulture, not a dove, to find land). Noah was the tenth in descent from Adam, and was six hundred years old when the biblical flood occurred, purportedly to cleanse the world of wickedness.

AND THE LORD said unto Noah, Come thou and all thy house into the ark; for thee have I seen righteous before me in this generation.

2 Of every clean beast thou shalt take to thee by sevens, the male and his female: and of beasts that are not clean by two, the male and his female.

3 Of fowls also of the air by sevens, the male and the female; to keep seed alive upon the face of all the earth.

4 For yet seven days, and I will cause it to rain upon the earth forty days and forty nights; and every living substance that I have made will I destroy from off the face of the earth.

5 And Noah did according unto all that the LORD commanded him.

6 And Noah was six hundred years old when the flood of waters was upon the earth.

7 And Noah went in, and his sons, and his wife, and his sons' wives with him, into the ark, because of the waters of the flood.

8 Of clean beasts, and of beasts that are not clean, and of fowls, and of every thing that creepeth upon the earth,

9 There went in two and two unto Noah into the ark, the male and the female, as God had commanded Noah.

10 And it came to pass after seven days, that the waters of the flood were upon the earth.

11 In the six hundredth year of Noah's life, in the second month, the seventeenth day of the month, the same day were all the fountains of the great deep broken up, and the windows of heaven were opened.

12 And the rain was upon the earth forty days and forty nights.

13 In the selfsame day entered Noah, and Shem, and Ham, and Japheth, the sons of Noah, and Noah's wife, and the three wives of his sons with them, into the ark;

14 They, and every beast after his kind, and all the cattle after their kind, and every creeping thing that creepeth upon the earth after his kind, and every fowl after his kind, every bird of every sort.

15 And they went in unto Noah into the ark, two and two of all flesh, wherein is the breath of life.

16 And they that went in, went in male and female of all flesh, as God had commanded him: and the LORD shut him in.

17 And the flood was forty days upon the earth; and the waters increased, and bare up the ark, and it was lift up above the earth.

18 And the waters prevailed, and were increased greatly upon the earth; and the ark went upon the face of the waters.

19 And the waters prevailed exceedingly upon the earth; and all the high hills, that were under the whole heaven, were covered.

20 Fifteen cubits upward did the waters prevail; and the mountains were covered.

21 And all flesh died that moved upon the earth, both of fowl, and of cattle, and of beast, and of every creeping thing that creepeth upon the earth, and every man:

22 All in whose nostrils was the breath of life, of all that was in the dry land, died.

23 And every living substance was destroyed which was upon the face of the ground, both man, and cattle, and the creeping things, and the fowl of the heaven; and they were destroyed from the earth: and Noah only remained alive, and they that were with him in the ark.

24 And the waters prevailed upon the earth a hundred and fifty days.

NOAH WOULD NOT GIVE
UP EVEN A SPLINTER

H oward Norman (1949–), author of *The Bird Artist* (1994) and *The Northern Lights* (1987), spent several months in the fall of 1977 in Churchill, Manitoba, translating Inuit legends told to him by Mark Nuqac, a native elder from the Baker Lake community identified by Knud Rasmussen in 1924 as Caribou Inuit. Nuqac's "Noah stories," as Norman called them, are first-contact myths, probably dating from the eighteenth century when Churchill was a Hudson's Bay Company trading post. In them, Noah's ark, filled with all manner of exotic animals, drifts into Hudson Bay and is stuck fast in the ice for the winter. "In a world of either feast or famine," writes Norman in his memoir, *In Fond Remembrance of Me* (2006), "imagine the sight to Inuit people as they looked up from their kayaks or sleds . . . of such potentially grand meals in the making." Apart from their humor, the myths provide a fascinating glimpse of the melding of European legend and Inuit storytelling.

IT WAS ALMOST winter. But the water had not turned to ice yet. After one storm a piece of driftwood was seen out at sea. The villagers gathered together and pointed at it. "It's on top of a wave now," one shouted. "It's disappeared now! It's on top of a wave now!" But that piece of driftwood didn't tumble in. "I hope we can have one more driftwood-fire before winter," a man said.

The next day, a storm. No driftwood. The next day, a storm—no driftwood. The next day, a storm—no driftwood. The next day someone shouted, "Look—out there!" Everyone saw a big wooden boat on top of a wave.

A storm hit hard. It was windy and there was sleet. When the storm ended, some villagers went looking for driftwood. No driftwood. But they found an animal washed up on the rocks. "What is that?" a man asked.

"It's not a seal," another man said. "It's not a polar bear. It's not—It's not—It's not—" People were confused.

"It's not a whale," another villager said. The animal had a very long neck. It was very tall. It had yellow skin and black spots. "No, that's not a seal," a woman said. In a short while every villager had gone out to look at this animal.

"It must have escaped from the wooden boat," a man said. "Where else could it have come from?" "Some of you haul it back out there," another woman said.

It took a lot of men to do this. They lay the tall animal across their kayaks. Paddling was not easy. There were rough waves and the spotted animal tilted the kayaks and kept them danger-ously low in the water. When they got to the big wooden boat, a man shouted up, "Hey—hey there!"

On deck appeared a man. He was standing next to a tall ani-mal with black spots. It had a long neck. Its skin was yellow—not paled by drowning, either. It had small horns. "Hey, there's another one!" a man shouted. "I wonder how it tastes?"

"What do you want?" the man shouted down.

"We've brought this dead animal back."

"It fell off my ark."

"What's that?"

"It's what my boat is called."

"What's your name?"

"Noah."

"What's this animal called?"

"A giraffe."

"Where you come from do you eat it?"

"Not my family."

"Is your family with you?"

"Yes—my wife. My son. My daughter."

"I bet they're inside the ark eating a giraffe."

The villagers in kayaks all laughed.

"No—no—there's only this one left alive," said Noah.

"Winter is coming in fast. You'll be without food. You better think abut eating that giraffe."

"No," said Noah.

"Well, the one lying across these kayaks is dead. We don't eat dead animals. Ravens might—foxes might, if the carcass is frozen. Crows do that, gulls do that."

"I don't want the dead giraffe," said Noah.

With that, the villagers pushed the giraffe into the sea. "Giraffe-sank-away," a man said.

It became winter. It was snowing. The ark was trapped in ice out there. Great hummocks of sea ice pushed up against it. Snow fell on the giraffe. Snow fell on Noah. In the village, people said, "Hey, Noah and his family must be hungry. If we have luck in hunting, let's bring them a seal." It was agreed. Some hunters walked out over the ice. They bent over seal breathing-holes. They caught many seals. All at once the dogs began to bark—all across the ice—echoes of dog barks—over there—over there—and the seal hunters looked around. "Hey—look there!" One shouted. Then from a different place on the ice men saw the other tall spotted giraffe walking out over the ice! It's long legs were not good for this. It collapsed and fell, it got up, it fell, it slid around. "Giraffe-on-the-ice," a hunter said.

"Let's get it!" another said.

So the men hunted the giraffe. When they got up close they threw spears and gaffing hooks and killed the giraffe. They fed some of it to their dogs. The dogs ate what they were given right away. The men hauled the rest back to their village. People there looked at the strange hooves. People ate some of the giraffe but didn't like it.

"Let's say thanks to Noah anyway," a woman said.

"He didn't give us this food," a hunter said. "We got it."

"His family must be starving," a woman said. "Bring him some of this animal, at least." So the hunters dragged the giraffe haunches out to the ark. "Hey, Noah!" one shouted out. "Here's some food to get you by for a while!"

"No!" Noah called down. "I see pieces of spotted hide still attached. We don't want it!"

"Noah, give us a plank of wood, we'll get you through the winter," a hunter said. We'll show you how to chisel through the ice for fishing. We'll show you how to lean over a seal breathing-hole. Just give us a plank of wood."

"No!" Noah shouted in anger. When he shouted he slid his hand across the rail of his ark. "Oh! Oh!" The villagers saw he had got a splinter in his thumb.

"Hey, Noah," a man said, "Just give us that splinter! We'll get you and your family through winter. Hey, come on! We can get that splinter out for you. We get splinters out all the time. Come on, it's just a tiny piece of wood. We get bone splinters out, other sorts . . . fish-bone splinters. We can spark a fire from just that splinter. Come on, we'll climb up and get that splinter out!"

Noah walked to the rail. He saw a villager climbing up. Noah struck this man with a long stick with bristles at the end. The man fell to the ice. "Hey—hey!" the man said. "Noah, what did you hit me with?"

"A broom," said Noah.

"Well, a bristle stuck in my face. I'm going to try and spark a fire from it!"

"Go away!" said Noah.

"Let us have the broom," said a man, "we'll get you through winter. Otherwise you'll starve."

"No, I sweep the ark with it every day," said Noah.

"Give us the broom, you won't have to sweep anymore!"

"No!"

The man Noah had struck with the broom said, "All right—winter can have you." The villagers all went home.

After the ice-break-up, some men paddled out to the ark. It was floating now, turning in slow circles, a lot of pieces of ice were still bumping against it. The men climbed onto the ark. "Hey—hey—Noah!" they shouted. They didn't hear any voice. They saw a lot of animal bones—all sizes—no animals. Then they saw Noah. He was lying down curled up. He was weeping. He was wearing a coat made of faded yellow skin with black spots. "One thumb splinter—one broom—one plank of wood," a man said, "it was a very tough winter. Where's your wife? Where's your son? Where's your daughter?"

"They ate the broom bristles and died," said Noah.

Some men pried up some planks and put them in their kayaks. They felt the ark begin to sink away. It was windy. It was raining hard. "Let's get this Noah to the village," a man said.

They took Noah and the planks to the village. They built a fire. Noah sat next to it. They fed him and kept him alive. He lived with them all summer and through the next winter. A few times they caught him walking out onto the ice. "He sees the ghosts of his family," a man said. It was true. Noah made a new broom and swept around. He ate, he swept, and every once in a while people caught him out on the ice. They brought Noah back.

One day in the middle of winter someone shouted, "It's Noah—he's out on the ice again! Hey—what are you doing?"

"I'm following my wife—look—up ahead—she's lost," he said.

One day later that winter someone shouted, "Hey—look! Noah, what are you doing out on the ice?"

"I'm following my daughter—look—up ahead—she's lost," he said.

On another day, Noah said, "I'm out on the ice because—look!—up ahead—it's my son—he's lost. I'm going after him to help."

Each time the villagers would tie Noah up with gut string and haul him back sliding over the ice. When they untied him in the village, he ate and got some strength back. Then he swept with the broom. He seldom slept. He swept and the villagers heard that sound. "No ark—but he sweeps," a woman said.

When next time the ice-break-up arrived the villagers decided that Noah had lived with them long enough. They went with him in the southerly direction. Then they gave him packets of food and sent him on his way. Planks from the ark washed up for a lot of summers. Not every time after a storm, but still there was driftwood, driftwood—driftwood. From that ark.

THE SLEEP AT SEA

HOMER

As ancient Greece was a seafaring nation, it makes sense that its greatest poet would provide a stirring account of a sea voyage. Nothing is known for certain of Homer's life except that he lived some time after the Trojan War, which, according to Herodotus, ended in 1250 BCE. Current scholarship holds that he lived either on the Ionian Islands or on the Turkish coast (his name means "hostage") in the mid-eighth century BCE, and that he was a transitional figure between Greek oral and written cultures: his two epic poems, the *Iliad* and the *Odyssey,* drew heavily from the oral tradition, but were written down and at least partly composed by another author. The *Odyssey* follows the ten-year return journey of its hero, Odysseus, to his home in Ithaca following the fall of Troy. In this excerpt, translated by Stephen Heighton, Odysseus and his crew depart from the island of Drepane, thought to be modern Corfu.

Now the crewmen sit to their oars in order and slip
the cable from the bollard hole and heave backwards
so their oarblades chop at the swell and churn up water
while over Odysseus sweet sleep irresistibly
falls so fathomless and sound it might almost be the sleep
of death itself. And the ship like a team of stallions
coursing to the crack of the lash with hoofs bounding
high and manes blown back like foam off the
    summits of waves
lunges along stern up and plunging as the riven
rollers close up crashing together in her wake
and she surges on so unrelenting not even a bird
quick as the falcon could have stayed abreast . . .
So she leaps on splitting the back combers bearing
a man godlike in his wisdom who has suffered years
of sorrow and turmoil until his heart grew weary
of scything a path home through his
    enemies or the furious
ocean; but now he sleeps profoundly, with all his griefs,
asleep at his side, forgotten.

THE SEAFARER

ANONYMOUS, TRANSLATED BY EZRA POUND

One of the oldest of Old English texts, "The Seafarer" is a poem of 124 lines preserved in the tenth-century *Exeter Book*, the most famous of three known collections of Anglo-Saxon poetry. The first half of the poem takes the form of an elegiac monologue by one who has endured years of hardship ("bitre breostceare") on the ice-cold sea ("iscealdne sae"). Despite the dangers, however, the aged Seafarer goes on to express his love for the ocean, and extols the courage and endurance such a life demands. This segment, translated by Ezra Pound (1885–1972), appeared in Pound's 1912 book *Ripostes*; although it varies from the original in many ways, it preserves the vividness of the narrative and the pang of longing for youthful adventures on the North Sea.

. . .

May I for my own self song's truth reckon,
Journey's jargon, how I in harsh days
Hardship endured oft.

Bitter breast-cares have I abided,
Known on my keel many a care's hold,
And dire sea-surge, and there I oft spent
Narrow nightwatch nigh the ship's head
While she tossed close to cliffs. Coldly afflicted,
My feet were by frost benumbed.
Chill its chains are; chafing sighs
Hew my heart round and hunger begot
Mere-weary mood. Lest man know not
That he on dry land loveliest liveth,
List how I, care-wretched, on ice-cold sea,
Weathered the winter, wretched outcast
Deprived of my kinsmen;
Hung with hard ice-flakes, where hail-scur flew,
There I heard naught save the harsh sea
And ice-cold wave, at whiles the swan cries,
Did for my games the gannet's clamour,
Sea-fowls, loudness was for me laughter,
The mews' singing all my mead-drink.
Storms, on the stone-cliffs beaten, fell on the stern
In icy feathers; full oft the eagle screamed
With spray on his pinion.

    Not any protector
May make merry man faring needy.
This he little believes, who aye in winsome life
Abides 'mid burghers some heavy business,
Wealthy and wine-flushed, how I weary oft

Must bide above brine.
Neareth nightshade, snoweth from north,
Frost froze the land, hail fell on earth then
Corn of the coldest. Nathless there knocketh now
The heart's thought that I on high streams
The salt-wavy tumult traverse alone.
Moaneth alway my mind's lust
That I fare forth, that I afar hence
Seek out a foreign fastness.
For this there's no mood-lofty man over earth's midst,
Not though he be given his good,
          but will have in his youth greed;
Nor his deed to the daring, nor his king to the faithful
But shall have his sorrow for sea-fare
Whatever his lord will.
He hath not heart for harping, nor in ring-having
Nor winsomeness to wife, nor world's delight
Nor any whit else save the wave's slash,
Yet longing comes upon him to fare forth on the water.
Bosque taketh blossom, cometh beauty of berries,
Fields to fairness, land fares brisker,
All this admonisheth man eager of mood,
The heart turns to travel so that he then thinks
On flood-ways to be far departing.
Cuckoo calleth with gloomy crying,
He singeth summerward, bodeth sorrow,
The bitter heart's blood. Burgher knows not—

He the prosperous man—what some perform
Where wandering them widest draweth.
So that but now my heart burst from my breast-lock,
My mood 'mid the mere-flood,
Over the whale's acre, would wander wide.
On earth's shelter cometh oft to me,
Eager and ready, the crying lone-flyer,
Whets for the whale-path the heart irresistibly,
O'er tracks of ocean; seeing that anyhow
My lord deems to me this dead life
On loan and on land, I believe not
That any earth-weal eternal standeth
Save there be somewhat calamitous
That, ere a man's tide go, turn it to twain.
Disease or oldness or sword-hate
Beats out the breath from doom-gripped body.
And for this, every earl whatever,
    for those speaking after—
Laud of the living, boasteth some last word,
That he will work ere he pass onward,
Frame on the fair earth 'gainst foes his malice,
Daring ado, . . .
So that all men shall honour him after
And his laud beyond them remain 'mid the English,
Aye, for ever, a lasting life's-blast,
Delight mid the doughty.
    Days little durable,

And all arrogance of earthen riches,
There come now no kings nor Cæsars
Nor gold-giving lords like those gone.
Howe'er in mirth most magnified,
Whoe'er lived in life most lordliest,
Drear all this excellence, delights undurable!
Waneth the watch, but the world holdeth.
Tomb hideth trouble. The blade is layed low.
Earthly glory ageth and seareth.
No man at all going the earth's gait,
But age fares against him, his face paleth,
Grey-haired he groaneth, knows gone companions,
Lordly men are to earth o'ergiven,
Nor may he then the flesh-cover, whose life ceaseth,
Nor eat the sweet nor feel the sorry,
Nor stir hand nor think in mid heart,
And though he strew the grave with gold,
His born brothers, their buried bodies
Be an unlikely treasure hoard.

A SCENE OF
HORRIBLE CALAMITIES

ANN SAUNDERS

Little is known of Ann Saunders that she doesn't tell us herself in *Narrative of the Shipwreck and Sufferings of Miss Ann Saunders,* a thirty-nine-page religious tract that she self-published in Providence, Rhode Island, in 1827, and from which this account of her oceanic ordeal is excerpted. She was born in Liverpool, England, in 1802, of "reputable" but poor parents; her father died when she was young, and she was placed in a foster home until she was eighteen. In January 1826, she sailed on the *Francis Mary,* a timber ship out of St. John, New Brunswick, bound for Liverpool, as maid to the wife of the ship's captain, John Kendall; one of the crew members, James Frier, was her fiancé. The ship's hull was stove in by a severe gale on February 1, but, because the ship was loaded with timber, it did not sink; passengers and crew survived until they were rescued on March 7. How they did so is the subject of Miss Saunders's graphic narrative.

WE ENJOYED FAVORABLE weather until about the 1st February, when a severe gale was experienced, which blew away some of the yards and spars of our vessel and washed away one of the boats off the deck and severely wounded some of the seamen. Early in the morning ensuing, the gale having somewhat abated, Mrs. Kendall and myself employed ourselves in dressing the wounds of the poor fellows that were most injured while those who had escaped injury were employed in clearing the deck of the broken spars, splicing and disentangling the rigging, so that in a few hours they were enabled again to make sail, and with the pleasing hope that they should encounter no more boisterous and contrary winds to impede their passage. But in this they were soon sadly disappointed, for on the 5th they were visited with a still more severe gale from ESE, which indeed caused the sea to run mountains high. The captain gave orders to his men to do everything in their power to do, for the safety of our lives. All sails were clewed up and the ship hove to, but the gale still increasing, after noon our vessel was struck by a tremendous sea, which swept from her decks almost every moveable article and washed one of the seamen overboard, who was providentially saved. A few moments after, the whole of the ship's stern was stove in. This was only the beginning of a scene of horrid calamities, doubly horrible to me, who had never before witnessed any thing so awful.

While the captain and officers of the ship were holding a consultation on deck what was best to be done for the preservation of our lives, Mrs. Kendall and myself were on our knees on the quarterdeck, engaged in earnest prayer to the Almighty God that he would in his tender mercy spare our lives.

The ensuing morning presented to our view an aspect the most dreary—not the least appearance of the gale abating, on the contrary it seemed to increase with redoubled vigor as the sea had rose to an alarming height and frequently dashed against the vessel with great violence. Little else was now thought of but the preservation of our lives. Exertions were made by the crew to save as much of the ship's provisions as was possible, and by breaking out the bow port they succeeded in saving fifty or sixty pounds of bread and a few pounds of cheese, which were stowed in the main top; to which place Mrs. Kendall and myself were conveyed, it being impossible for us to remain below, the cabin being nearly filled with water and almost every sea breaking over us. The night approached with all its dismal horrors—the horizon was obscured by black and angry-looking clouds, and about midnight the rain commenced falling in torrents, attended with frightful peals of thunder and unremitting streams of lightning.

Daylight returned, but only to present to our view an additional scene of horror—one of the poor seamen, overcome by fatigue, was discovered hanging lifeless by some part of the rigging. His mortal remains were committed to the deep. As this was the first instance of entombing a human body in the ocean that I had ever witnessed, the melancholy scene made a deep impression on my mind, as I expected such eventually would be my own fate.

At 6 AM our depressed spirits were a little revived by the appearance of a sail standing toward us; which proved to be an American, who remained in company with us until the next morning; when, in consequence of the roughness of the sea, being unable to afford us any assistance, they left us.

It would be impossible for me to attempt to describe the feelings of all on board at this moment, on seeing so unexpectedly vanish the pleasing hope of being rescued by this vessel from our perilous situation. As the only human means to prolong our miserable existence a tent of spare canvass was erected by the ship's crew on the forecastle, and all on board put on the short allowance of a quarter of a biscuit a day. On the 8th February (the gale still continuing) a brig was seen to leeward but at a great distance, and in the afternoon the same brig was seen to windward. Captain Kendall ordered a signal of distress to be made and we soon had the satisfaction to see the brig approach us within hail and inquire very distinctly of Captain Kendall how long we had been in that situation and what he intended to do—if he intended leaving the ship? to which he replied "Yes, with God's assistance." But night approaching and the gale still prevailing to that degree that no boat could have floated in the water, we saw no more of the brig!

All on board were now reduced to the most deplorable state imaginable. Our miserable bodies were gradually perishing and the disconsolate spirits of the poor sailors (who were probably, like too many of their seafaring brethren, strangers to prayer) were overpowered by the horrible prospects of starving without any appearance of relief.

February the 11th another vessel was discovered at the northward, and the signal of distress again made, but without any effect, as she did not alter her course and was soon out of sight. We had now arrived at an awful crisis—our provisions were all consumed and hunger and thirst began to select their victims. On the 12th James Clarke, a seaman, died of no other complaint (as was judged) than the weakness caused by famine; whose body, after reading prayers, was committed to the deep. And on the 22nd John Wilson, another seaman, fell a victim of starvation.

As the calls of hunger had now become too importunate to be resisted, it is a fact, although shocking to relate, that we were reduced to the awful extremity to attempt to support our feeble bodies a while longer by subsisting on the dead body of the deceased—it was cut into slices, then washed in salt water, and after being exposed to and dried in the sun, was apportioned to each of the miserable survivors, who partook of it as a sweet morsel. From this revolting food I abstained for twenty-four hours, when I too was compelled by hunger to follow their example. This is indeed the height of misery, yet such was our deplorable case. We eyed each other with mournful and melancholy looks, as may be supposed of people perishing with hunger and thirst; by all of whom it was now perceived that we had nothing to hope from human aid but only from the mercy of the Almighty, whose ways are unsearchable—nor did I fail almost constantly to implore His mercy.

On the 23rd J. Moore, another seaman, died, whose body was committed to the deep after taking therefrom the liver and heart, which was reserved for our subsistence. And in the course of twelve days after (during which our miseries continued without any alleviation) the following persons fell victims to fatigue and hunger, to wit: Henry Davis and John Jones, cabin boys; James Frier, cook; Alexander Kelly, Daniel Jones, John Hutchinson and John James, seamen. The heart-piercing lamentations of these poor creatures (dying for want of sustenance) was distressing beyond conception. Some of them expired raving mad, crying out lamentably for water. Hutchinson, who, it appeared, had left a numerous family in Europe, talked to his wife and children as if they were present, repeating the names of the latter, and begged of them to be kind to their poor mother who, he represented, was about to be separated from him forever. Jones became delirious two or three days before his death and in his ravings reproached his wife and children as well as his dying companions present with being the authors of his extreme sufferings by depriving him of food and in refusing him even a single drop of water with which to moisten his parched lips. And, indeed, such now was the thirst of those who were but in little better condition that they were driven to the melancholy distressful horrid act (to procure their blood) of cutting the throats of their deceased companions a moment after the breath of life had left their bodies!

In the untimely exit of no one of the unhappy sufferers was I so sensibly affected as that of the unfortunate youth, James Frier—for in the welfare of none on board did I feel myself so immediately interested. I have already stated that with this ill-fated young man I became intimately acquainted in Liverpool. To me he had early made protestations of love and more than once intimated an inclination to select me as the partner of his bosom; and never had I any reason to doubt his sincerity. It was partly by his solicitations that I had been induced to comply with the wishes of Mrs. Kendall to accompany her in this unfortunate voyage, in the course of which, by frequent interviews, my attachment for this unfortunate youth was rather increased than diminished. And before this dreadful calamity befell us he had obtained my consent and we had mutually agreed and avowed to each other our determination to unite in marriage as soon as we should reach our destined port. Judge then, my female readers (for it is you that can best judge) what must have been my feelings, to see a youth for whom I had formed an indissoluble attachment—him with whom I expected so soon to be joined in wedlock and to spend the remainder of my days—expiring before my eyes for the want of that sustenance which nature requires for the support of life and which it was not in my power to afford him. And myself at the same moment so far reduced by hunger and thirst as to be driven to the horrid alternative to preserve my own life (O God of Heaven! the lamentable fact is known to thee, and why should I attempt to conceal it from the world?) to plead my claim to the greater portion of his precious blood as it oozed half congealed from the wound inflicted upon his lifeless body! Oh, this was a bitter cup indeed! But it was God's will that it should not pass me—and God's will must be done. O, it was a chastening rod that has been the means, I trust, of weaning me forever from all the vain enjoyments of this frail world.

"Think, mortal," says the poet, "what it is to die," but I would add, think how distressing it must be to see those whom we tenderly love, die before our eyes. One who was in the bloom and vigor of life but a few days previous was thus, in an unexpected manner, ushered into the unseen world.

While almost every other person on board were rendered so weak by their extreme sufferings and deprivations as to be unable to stand upon their feet or even to detach from the lifeless bodies of their unfortunate companions that food which was now nature's only support, the Almighty, in mercy to me, endowed me with not only the strength and ability to exhort the poor wretches to unite in prayer and to prepare their precious souls for eternity, but also to perform this office for them, for which purpose I constantly carried about with me a knife, with which I daily detached and presented each with a proportionable quantity of this their only food. My poor unfortunate female companion, Mrs. Kendall, seemed too to enjoy with me a share of God's great mercy. But the reader may judge to what extremity of want we all must have been driven when she, two days before we were relieved, was compelled by hunger to eat the brains of one of the seamen, declaring in the meantime that it was the most delicious thing she ever tasted.

About the 26th February an English brig hove in sight, on which the usual signals of distress were made and, although the winds had become less boisterous and the sea more smooth, to our inexpressible grief she did not approach to afford us any assistance. Our longing eyes followed her until she was out of sight leaving us in a situation doubly calamitous from our disappointment in not receiving the relief which appeared so near. Our hopes vanished with the brig and from the highest summit of expectation they now sunk into a state of the most dismal despair. Nature indeed seemed now to have abandoned her functions. Never could human beings be reduced to a more wretched situation. More than two thirds of the crew had already perished and the surviving few—weak, distracted, and destitute of almost everything—envied the fate of those whose lifeless corpses no longer wanted sustenance. The sense of hunger was almost lost, but a parching thirst consumed our vitals. Our mouths had become so dry for want of moisture for three or four days that we were obliged to wash them every few hours with salt water to prevent our lips glueing together.

Early in the morning of the 7th March a sail was discovered to windward. The ship's crew (with my assistance) made all the signals of distress that the little remaining strength of their bodies would enable them to do. They were indeed the last efforts of expiring nature. But, praised be God, the hour of our deliverance had now arrived. The ship was soon within hail, which proved to be His Majesty's Ship *Blonde*, Lord Byron, when her boat was manned and sent to our relief.

It would be in vain for me to attempt to describe our feeling at this moment or those manifested by our deliverers when they discovered who we were and what our miserable situation;

and that they had arrived in season to rescue six of their fellow creatures from a most awful but certain death. My companions in misery, who for three or four of the preceding days had been only able to crawl about the deck upon their hands and knees, now became so animated at the prospect of relief as to raise themselves erect and with uplifted hands returned thanks to ·their Almighty preserver.

When relieved, but a small part of the body of the last person deceased remained, and this I had cut as usual into slices and spread on the quarterdeck; which being noticed by the lieutenant of the *Blonde* (who with others had been dispatched from the ship to our relief) and before we had time to state to him to what extremities we had been driven, he observed, "You have yet, I perceive, fresh meat." But his horror can be better conceived than described when he was informed that what he saw was the remains of the dead body of one of our unfortunate companions and that on this, our only remaining food, it was our intention to have put ourselves on an allowance the ensuing evening had not unerring Providence directed him to our relief.

PHOSPHORESCENCE
OF THE SEA

CHARLES DARWIN

C harles Darwin (1809–1882) began his famous five-year voyage aboard the HMS *Beagle* in 1831, when he sailed from Plymouth Sound, down the eastern coast of South America, through the Straits of Magellan, and back to England. It was undoubtedly one of the most significant voyages in scientific history, for it was during these long, solitary hours that Darwin made the observations that resulted in his theory of evolution based on the distribution and abundance of species. Much of his research was conducted on land, but even while at sea, Darwin made careful notes of everything he saw. The following account of a curious marine phenomenon was recorded while the *Beagle* was sailing between latitudes 56 and 57, south of Cape Horn, and is taken from Darwin's first book, *Journal of Researches*, published in 1839.

. . .

WHILE SAILING IN these latitudes on one very dark night, the sea presented a wonderful and most beautiful spectacle. There

43

was a fresh breeze, and every part of the surface, which during the day is seen as foam, now glowed with a pale light. The vessel drove before her bows two billows of liquid phosphorus, and in her wake she was followed by a milky train. As far as the eye reached, the crest of every wave was bright, and the sky above the horizon, from the reflected glare of these livid flames, was not so utterly obscure, as over the rest of the heavens.

As we proceed further southward, the sea is seldom phosphorescent; and off Cape Horn, I do not recollect more than once having seen it so, and then it was far from being brilliant. This circumstance probably has a close connexion with the scarcity of organic beings in that part of the ocean. After the elaborate paper by Ehrenberg on the phosphorescence of the sea, it is almost superfluous on my part to make any observations on the subject. I may however add that the same torn and irregular particles of gelatinous matter, described by Ehrenberg, seem in the southern as well as in the northern hemisphere to be the common cause of this phenomenon. The particles were so minute as easily to pass through fine gauze; yet many were distinctly visible by the naked eye. The water when placed in a tumbler and agitated gave out sparks, but a small portion in a watch-glass scarcely ever was luminous. Ehrenberg states that these particles all retain a certain degree of irritability. My observations, some of which were made directly after taking up the water, would give a different result. I may also mention that having used the net during one night I allowed it to become partially dry, and having occasion twelve hours afterwards to employ it again, I found the whole surface sparkled as brightly as when first taken out of the water. It does not appear probable in this case that the particles could have remained alive. I remark also in my notes that having kept a Medusa of the genus Dianæa till it was dead, the water in which it was placed became luminous. When the waves scintillate with bright green sparks, I believe it is generally owing to minute crustacea. But there can be no doubt that the very many other pelagic animals, when alive, are phosphorescent.

On two occasions I have observed the sea luminous at considerable depths beneath the surface. Near the mouth of the Plata some circular and oval patches, from two to four yards in diameter, and with defined outlines, shone with a steady, but pale light, while the surrounding water only gave out a few sparks. The appearance resembled the reflection of the moon, or some luminous body, for the edges were sinuous from the undulation of the surface. The ship, which drew thirteen feet of water, passed over, without disturbing, these patches. Therefore we must suppose that some animals were congregated together at greater depth than the bottom of the vessel.

Near Fernando Noronha the sea gave out light in flashes. The appearance was very similar to that which might be expected from a large fish moving rapidly through a luminous fluid. To this cause the sailors attributed it; at the time, however, I entertained some doubts, on account of the frequency and rapidity of the flashes. With respect to any general observations, I have already stated that the display is very much more common in warm than in cold countries. I have sometimes imagined that a disturbed electrical condition of the atmosphere was most favourable to its production. Certainly I think the sea is most luminous after a few days of more calm weather than ordinary, during which time it has swarmed with various animals. Observing that the water charged with gelatinous particles is in an impure state, and that the luminous appearance in all common cases is produced by the agitation of the fluid in contact with the atmosphere, I have always been inclined to consider that the phosphorescence was the result of the decomposition of the organic particles, by which process (one is tempted almost to call it a kind of respiration) the ocean becomes purified.

THE PACIFIC

HERMAN MELVILLE

Born in New York City to a merchant family, Herman Melville (1819–1891) sailed to Liverpool at the age of nineteen and later joined a whaling expedition to the South Seas, during which he jumped ship and lived among the Typee cannibals in the Marquesas. He "has the strange, uncanny magic of sea-creatures," D.H. Lawrence wrote of him, "and some of their repulsiveness . . . There is something slithery about him." His early novels—*Typee* (1846), *Omoo* (1847), and *Mardi* (1849)—brought him a measure of fame, but his masterpiece, *Moby Dick* (1851), excerpted here, was not well received, although it has since been recognized as a cornerstone of American literature. As this description of the Pacific Ocean attests, the novel combines vividly accomplished narrative fiction with passages of almost postmodern documentary nonfiction.

. . .

WHEN GLIDING BY the Bashee isles we emerged at last upon the great South Sea; were it not for other things, I could have greeted my dear Pacific with uncounted thanks, for now the long supplication of my youth was answered; that serene ocean rolled eastwards from me a thousand leagues of blue.

There is, one knows not what sweet mystery about this sea, whose gently awful stirrings seem to speak of some hidden soul beneath; like those fabled undulations of the Ephesian sod over the buried Evangelist St. John. And meet it is that over these sea-pastures, wide-rolling watery prairies and Potters' Fields of all four continents, the waves should rise and fall, and ebb and flow unceasingly; for here, millions of mixed shades and shadows, drowned dreams, somnambulisms, reveries; all that we call lives and souls, like dreaming, dreaming, still; tossing like slumberers in their beds; the ever-rolling waves but made so by their restlessness.

To any meditative Magian rover, this serene Pacific, once beheld, must ever after be the sea of his adoption. It rolls the mid-most waters of the world, the Indian ocean and Atlantic being but its arms. The same waves wash the moles of the new-built Californian towns, but yesterday planted by the recentest race of men, and lave the faded but still gorgeous skirts of Asiatic lands, older than Abraham; while all between float milky-ways of coral isles, and low-lying, endless, unknown Archipelagoes, and impenetrable Japans. Thus this mysterious, divine Pacific zones the world's whole bulk about; makes all coasts one bay to it; seems the tide-beating heart of earth. Lifted by those eternal swells, you needs must own the seductive god, bowing your head to Pan.

But few thoughts of Pan stirred Ahab's brain, as standing like an iron statue at his accustomed place beside the mizzen rigging, with one nostril he unthinkingly snuffed the sugary musk from the Bashee isles (in whose sweet woods mild lovers must be walking), and with the other consciously inhaled the salt breath of the new found sea; that sea in which the hated white whale must even then be swimming. Launched at length upon these almost final waters, and gliding towards the Japanese cruising-ground, the old man's purpose intensified itself. His firm lips met like the lips of a vice; the Delta of his forehead's veins swelled like overladen brooks; in his very sleep, his ringing cry ran through the vaulted hull, "Stern all! the white whale spouts thick blood."

PIRATES AND OTHER
COMPANIONS

JOSHUA SLOCUM

The intrepid Joshua Slocum (1844–1909) was born in Annapolis County, Nova Scotia, and at age fourteen became a cook on a fishing schooner; ten years later he was in command of a merchant vessel sailing between San Francisco and China. After 1882, he owned and commanded a succession of merchant vessels, including the *Liberdade*, which he sailed from Brazil to Washington, D.C.; his memoir of that adventure was published in 1890. Two years later, he acquired and refurbished the *Spray*, a derelict oyster sloop, and on April 24, 1895, at the age of fifty-one, departed from Boston to sail around the world. He came into Newport, Rhode Island, on June 27, 1898, the first person to have circumnavigated the globe single-handedly. His account of that historic voyage, *Sailing Alone Around the World*, from which this excerpt is taken, was published in 1900. In 1909, Slocum set out on another solo voyage aboard the *Spray*, this one to South America. He was never heard from again.

MONDAY, AUGUST 25, the *Spray* sailed from Gibraltar, well repaid for whatever deviation she had made from a direct course to reach the place. A tug belonging to her Majesty towed the sloop into the steady breeze clear of the mount, where her sails caught a volant wind, which carried her once more to the Atlantic, where it rose rapidly to a furious gale. My plan was, in going down this coast, to haul offshore, well clear of the land, which hereabouts is the home of pirates; but I had hardly accomplished this when I perceived a felucca making out of the nearest port, and finally following in the wake of the *Spray*. Now, my course to Gibraltar had been taken with a view to proceed up the Mediterranean Sea, through the Suez Canal, down the Red Sea, and east about, instead of a western route, which I finally adopted. By officers of vast experience in navigating these seas, I was influenced to make the change. Longshore pirates on both coasts being numerous, I could not afford to make light of the advice. But here I was, after all, evidently in the midst of pirates and thieves! I changed my course; the felucca did the same, both vessels sailing very fast, but the distance growing less and less between us. The *Spray* was doing nobly; she was even more than at her best; but, in spite of all I could do, she would broach now and then. She was carrying too much sail for safety. I must reef or be dismasted and lose all, pirate or no pirate. I must reef, even if I had to grapple with him for my life.

I was not long in reefing the mainsail and sweating it up— probably not more than fifteen minutes; but the felucca had in the meantime so shortened the distance between us that I now saw the tuft of hair on the heads of the crew—by which, it is said, Mohammed will pull the villains up into heaven—and they were coming on like the wind. From what I could clearly make out now, I felt them to be the sons of generations of pirates, and I saw by their movements that they were now preparing to strike a blow. The exultation on their faces, however, was changed in an instant to a look of fear and rage. Their craft, with too much sail on, broached to on the crest of a great wave. This one great sea changed the aspect of affairs suddenly as the flash of a gun. Three minutes later the same wave overtook the *Spray* and shook her in every timber. At the same moment the sheet-strop parted, and away went the main-boom, broken short at the rigging. Impulsively I sprang to the jib-halyards and down-haul, and instantly downed the jib. The head-sail being off, and the helm put hard down, the sloop came in the wind with a bound. While shivering there, but a moment though it was, I got the mainsail down and secured inboard, broken boom and all. How I got the boom in before the sail was torn I hardly know; but not a stitch of it was broken. The mainsail being secured, I hoisted away the jib, and, without looking round, stepped quickly to the cabin and snatched down my loaded rifle and cartridges at hand; for I made mental calculations that the pirate would by this time have recovered his course and be close aboard, and that when I saw him it would be better for me to be looking at him along the barrel of a gun. The piece was at my shoulder when I peered into the mist, but there was no pirate within a mile. The wave and squall that carried away my boom dismasted the felucca outright. I perceived his thieving crew, some dozen or more of them, struggling to recover their rigging from the sea. Allah blacken their faces!

I sailed comfortably on under the jib and fore-stay-sail, which I now set. I fished the boom and furled the sail snug for the night; then hauled the sloop's head two points offshore to allow for the set of current and heavy rollers toward the land. This gave me the wind three points on the starboard quarter and a steady pull in the headsails. By the time I had things in this order it was dark, and a flying-fish had already fallen on deck. I took him below for my supper, but found myself too tired to cook, or even to eat a thing already prepared. I do not remember to have been more tired before or since in all my life than I was at the finish of that day. Too fatigued to sleep, I rolled about with the motion of the vessel till near midnight, when I made shift to dress my fish and prepare a dish of tea. I fully realized now, if I had not before, that the voyage ahead would call for exertions ardent and lasting. On August 27 nothing could be seen of the Moor, or his country either, except two peaks, away in the east through the clear atmosphere of morning. Soon after the sun rose even these were obscured by haze, much to my satisfaction.

The wind, for a few days following my escape from the pirates, blew a steady but moderate gale, and the sea, though agitated into long rollers, was not uncomfortably rough or dangerous, and while sitting in my cabin I could hardly realize that any sea was running at all, so easy was the long, swinging motion of the sloop over the waves. All distracting uneasiness and excitement being now over, I was once more alone with myself in the realization that I was on the mighty sea and in the hands of the elements. But I was happy, and was becoming more and more interested in the voyage.

Columbus, in the *Santa Maria*, sailing these seas more than four hundred years before, was not so happy as I, nor so sure of success in what he had undertaken. His first troubles at sea had already begun. His crew had managed, by foul play or otherwise, to break the ship's rudder while running before probably just such a gale as the *Spray* had passed through; and there was dissension on the *Santa Maria*, something that was unknown on the *Spray*.

After three days of squalls and shifting winds I threw myself down to rest and sleep, while, with helm lashed, the sloop sailed steadily on her course.

September 1, in the early morning, land-clouds rising ahead told of the Canary Islands not far away. A change in the weather came next day: storm-clouds stretched their arms across the sky; from the east, to all appearances, might come a fierce harmattan, or from the south might come the fierce hurricane. Every point of the compass threatened a wild storm. My attention was turned to reefing sails, and no time was to be lost over it, either, for the sea in a moment was confusion itself, and I was glad to head the sloop three points or more away from her true course that she might ride safely over the waves. I was now scudding

her for the channel between Africa and the island of Fuerteventura, the easternmost of the Canary Islands, for which I was on
the lookout. At 2 PM, the weather becoming suddenly fine, the
island stood in view, already abeam to starboard, and not more
than seven miles off. Fuerteventura is twenty-seven hundred
feet high, and in fine weather is visible many leagues away.

The wind freshened in the night, and the *Spray* had a fine
run through the channel. By daylight, September 3, she was
twenty-five miles clear of all the islands, when a calm ensued,
which was the precursor of another gale of wind that soon came
on, bringing with it dust from the African shore. It howled dis-
mally while it lasted, and though it was not the season of the
harmattan, the sea in the course of an hour was discolored with
a reddish-brown dust. The air remained thick with flying dust
all the afternoon, but the wind, veering northwest at night,
swept it back to land, and afforded the *Spray* once more a clear
sky. Her mast now bent under a strong, steady pressure, and her
bellying sail swept the sea as she rolled scuppers under, court-
seying to the waves. These rolling waves thrilled me as they
tossed my ship, passing quickly under her keel. This was grand
sailing. September 4, the wind, still fresh, blew from the north-
northeast, and the sea surged along with the sloop. About noon
a steamship, a bullock-droger, from the river Plate hove in sight,
steering northeast, and making bad weather of it. I signalled her,
but got no answer. She was plunging into the head sea and rolling in a most astonishing manner, and from the way she yawed
one might have said that a wild steer was at the helm.

On the morning of September 6 I found three flying-fish on deck, and a fourth one down the fore-scuttle as close as possible to the frying-pan. It was the best haul yet, and afforded me a sumptuous breakfast and dinner.

The *Spray* had now settled down to the trade-winds and to the business of her voyage. Later in the day another droger hove in sight, rolling as badly as her predecessor. I threw out no flag to this one, but got the worst of it for passing under her lee. She was, indeed, a stale one! And the poor cattle, how they bellowed! The time was when ships passing one another at sea backed their topsails and had a "gam," and on parting fired guns; but those good old days have gone. People have hardly time nowadays to speak even on the broad ocean, where news is news, and as for a salute of guns, they cannot afford the powder. There are no poetry-enshrined freighters on the sea now; it is a prosy life when we have no time to bid one another good morning.

My ship, running now in the full swing of the trades, left me days to myself for rest and recuperation. I employed the time in reading and writing, or in whatever I found to do about the rigging and the sails to keep them all in order. The cooking was always done quickly, and was a small matter, as the bill of fare consisted mostly of flying-fish, hot biscuits and butter, potatoes, coffee and cream—dishes readily prepared.

On September 10 the *Spray* passed the island of St. Antonio, the northwesternmost of the Cape Verdes, close aboard. The landfall was wonderfully true, considering that no observations for longitude had been made. The wind, northeast, as the sloop drew by the island, was very squally, but I reefed her sails snug, and steered broad from the highland of blustering St. Antonio. Then leaving the Cape Verde Islands out of sight astern, I found myself once more sailing a lonely sea and in a solitude supreme all around. When I slept I dreamed that I was alone. This feeling never left me; but, sleeping or waking, I seemed always to know the position of the sloop, and I saw my vessel moving across the chart, which became a picture before me.

One night while I sat in the cabin under this spell, the profound stillness all about was broken by human voices alongside! I sprang instantly to the deck, startled beyond my power to tell. Passing close under lee, like an apparition, was a white bark under full sail. The sailors on board of her were hauling on ropes to brace the yards, which just cleared the sloop's mast as she swept by. No one hailed from the white-winged flier, but I heard some one on board say that he saw lights on the sloop, and that he made her out to be a fisherman. I sat long on the starlit deck that night, thinking of ships, and watching the constellations on their voyage.

On the following day, September 13, a large four-masted ship passed some distance to windward, heading north.

The sloop was now rapidly drawing toward the region of doldrums, and the force of the trade-winds was lessening. I could see by the ripples that a counter-current had set in. This I estimated to be about sixteen miles a day. In the heart of the counter-stream the rate was more than that setting eastward.

September 14 a lofty three-masted ship, heading north, was seen from the masthead. Neither this ship nor the one seen yesterday was within signal distance, yet it was good even to see them. On the following day heavy rain-clouds rose in the south, obscuring the sun; this was ominous of doldrums. On the 16th the *Spray* entered this gloomy region, to battle with squalls and to be harassed by fitful calms; for this is the state of the elements between the northeast and the southeast trades, where each wind, struggling in turn for mastery, expends its force whirling about in all directions. Making this still more trying to one's nerve and patience, the sea was tossed into confused cross-lumps and fretted by eddying currents. As if something more were needed to complete a sailor's discomfort in this state, the rain poured down in torrents day and night. The *Spray* struggled and tossed for ten days, making only three hundred miles on her course in all that time. I didn't say anything!

On September 23 the fine schooner *Nantasket* of Boston, from Bear River, for the river Plate, lumber-laden, and just through the doldrums, came up with the *Spray*, and her captain passing a few words, she sailed on. Being much fouled on the bottom by shell-fish, she drew along with her fishes which had been following the *Spray*, which was less provided with that sort of food. Fishes will always follow a foul ship. A barnacle-grown log adrift has the same attraction for deep-sea fishes. One of this little school of deserters was a dolphin that had followed the *Spray* about a thousand miles, and had been content to eat scraps of food thrown overboard from my table; for, having been wounded, it could not dart through the sea to prey on other fishes. I had become accustomed to seeing the dolphin, which I knew by its scars, and missed it whenever it took occasional excursions away from the sloop. One day, after it had been off some hours, it returned in company with three yellowtails, a sort of cousin to the dolphin. This little school kept together, except when in danger and when foraging about the sea. Their lives were often threatened by hungry sharks that came round the vessel, and more than once they had narrow escapes. Their mode of escape interested me greatly, and I passed hours watching them. They would dart away, each in a different direction, so that the wolf of the sea, the shark, pursuing one, would be led away from the others; then after a while they would all return and rendezvous under one side or the other of the sloop. Twice their pursuers were diverted by a tin pan, which I towed astern of the sloop, and which was mistaken for a bright fish; and while turning, in the peculiar way that sharks have when about to devour their prey, I shot them through the head.

Their precarious life seemed to concern the yellowtails very little, if at all. All living beings, without doubt, are afraid of death. Nevertheless, some of the species I saw huddle together as though they knew they were created for the larger fishes, and wished to give the least possible trouble to their captors. I have seen, on the other hand, whales swimming in a circle around a school of herrings, and with mighty exertion "bunching" them together in a whirlpool set in motion by their flukes, and when the small fry were all whirled nicely together, one or the other of the leviathans, lunging through the centre with open jaws, take in a boat-load or so at a single mouthful. Off the Cape of Good Hope I saw schools of sardines or other small fish being treated in this way by great numbers of cavally-fish. There was not the slightest chance of escape for the sardines, while the cavally circled round and round, feeding from the edge of the mass. It was interesting to note how rapidly the small fry disappeared; and though it was repeated before my eyes over and over, I could hardly perceive the capture of a single sardine, so dexterously was it done.

Along the equatorial limit of the southeast trade-winds the air was heavily charged with electricity, and there was much thunder and lightning. It was hereabout I remembered that, a few years before, the American ship *Alert* was destroyed by lightning. Her people, by wonderful good fortune, were rescued on the same day and brought to Pernambuco, where I then met them.

On September 25, in the latitude of 5 degrees N, longitude 26 degrees 30′ w, I spoke the ship *North Star* of London. The great ship was out forty-eight days from Norfolk, Virginia, and was bound for Rio, where we met again about two months later. The *Spray* was now thirty days from Gibraltar.

The *Spray*'s next companion of the voyage was a swordfish, that swam alongside, showing its tall fin out of the water, till I made a stir for my harpoon, when it hauled its black flag down and disappeared. September 30, at half-past eleven in the morning, the *Spray* crossed the equator in longitude 29 degrees 30′ w. At noon she was two miles south of the line. The southeast trade-winds, met, rather light, in about 4 degrees N, gave her sails now a stiff full breeze, sending her handsomely over the sea toward the coast of Brazil, where on October 5, just north of Olinda Point, without further incident, she made the land, casting anchor in Pernambuco harbor about noon: forty days from Gibraltar, and all well on board. Did I tire of the voyage in all that time? Not a bit of it! I was never in better trim in all my life, and was eager for the more perilous experience of rounding the Horn.

PILOTS

JOSEPH CONRAD

Józef Teodor Konrad Korzeniowski (1857–1924) was born in the Russian Ukraine. His parents, members of the Polish nobility, were exiled to the northern Russian city of Vologda, and after their deaths, Conrad was sent to live with his uncle in Kraków. In 1874 he left Poland for Marseille, partly to avoid conscription into the Russian army, but also to fulfill a burning ambition to go to sea. Although he started as a deckhand, he eventually became a master mariner and spent most of his time in the tropics. While in the Congo, he began writing *Almayer's Folly*, which was published in 1895. Many of his novels, including *The Nigger of the "Narcissus"* (1897), *Lord Jim* (1900), and *Nostromo* (1904), reflect his experiences on the high seas, and his memoir, *A Personal Record* (1912), from which the following passage is taken, traces his love of ship life to the simple, kindly harbor pilots he apprenticed with while living in Marseille.

. . .

THE PATRON OF the Third Company (there were five companies of pilots at that time, I believe) is the brother-in-law of my friend Solary (Baptistin), a broad-shouldered, deep-chested man of forty, with a keen, frank glance which always seeks your eyes. He greets me by a low, hearty *"Hé, l'ami. Comment va?"* With his clipped moustache and massive open face, energetic and at the same time placid in expression, he is a fine specimen of the southerner of the calm type. For there is such a type in which the volatile southern passion is transmuted into solid force. He is fair, but no one could mistake him for a man of the north even by the dim gleam of the lantern standing on the quay. He is worth a dozen of your ordinary Normans or Bretons, but then, in the whole immense sweep of the Mediterranean shores, you could not find half a dozen men of his stamp.

Standing by the tiller, he pulls out his watch from under a thick jacket and bends his head over it in the light cast into the boat. Time's up. His pleasant voice commands, in a quiet undertone, *"Larguez."* A suddenly projected arm snatches the lantern off the quay—and, warped along by a line at first, then with the regular tug of four heavy sweeps in the bow, the big half-decked boat full of men glides out of the black, breathless shadow of the Fort. The open water of the *avant-port* glitters under the moon as if sown over with millions of sequins, and the long white breakwater shines like a thick bar of solid silver. With a quick rattle of blocks and one single silky swish, the sail is filled by a little breeze keen enough to have come straight down from the frozen moon, and the boat, after the clatter of the hauled-in sweeps, seems to stand at rest, surrounded by a mysterious whispering so faint and unearthly that it may be the rustling of the brilliant, overpowering moonrays breaking like a rain-shower upon the hard, smooth, shadowless sea.

I may well remember that last night spent with the pilots of the Third Company. I have known the spell of moonlight since, on various seas and coasts—coasts of forests, of rocks, of sand dunes—but no magic so perfect in its revelation of unsuspected character, as though one were allowed to look upon the mystic nature of material things. For hours I suppose no word was spoken in that boat. The pilots seated in two rows facing each other dozed with their arms folded and their chins resting upon their breasts. They displayed a great variety of caps: cloth, wool, leather, ear-flaps, tassels, with a picturesque round *béret* or two pulled down over the brows; and one grandfather, with a shaved, bony face and a great beak of a nose, had a cloak with a hood which made him look in our midst like a cowled monk being carried off goodness knows where by that silent company of seamen—quiet enough to be dead.

My fingers itched for the tiller, and in due course my friend, the *patron,* surrendered it to me in the same spirit in which the family coachman lets a boy hold the reins on an easy bit of road. There was a great solitude around us; the islets ahead, Monte Cristo and the Château d'If in full light, seemed to float toward us—so steady, so imperceptible was the progress of our boat. "Keep her in the furrow of the moon," the patron directed me in a quiet murmur, sitting down ponderously in the stern-sheets and reaching for his pipe.

The pilot station in weather like this was only a mile or two to the westward of the islets; and presently, as we approached the spot, the boat we were going to relieve swam into our view suddenly, on her way home, cutting black and sinister into the wake of the moon under a sable wing, while to them our sail must have been a vision of white and dazzling radiance. Without altering the course a hair's-breadth, we slipped by each other within an oar's-length. A drawling, sardonic hail came out of her. Instantly, as if by magic, our dozing pilots got on their feet in a body. An incredible babel of bantering shouts burst out, a jocular, passionate, voluble chatter, which lasted till the boats were stern to stern, theirs all bright now and with a shining sail to our eye, we turned all black to their vision, and drew away from them under a sable wing. That extraordinary uproar died away almost as suddenly as it had begun; first one had enough of it and sat down, then another, then three or four together, and when all had left off with mutters and growling half-laughs the sound of hearty chuckling became audible, persistent, unnoticed. The cowled grandfather was very much entertained somewhere within his hood.

He had not joined in the shouting of jokes, neither had he moved the least bit. He had remained quietly in his place against the foot of the mast. I had been given to understand long before that he had the rating of a second-class able seaman *(matelot léger)* in the fleet which sailed from Toulon for the conquest of Algeria in the year of grace 1830. And, indeed, I had seen and examined one of the buttons of his old brown patched coat, the only brass button of the miscellaneous lot, flat and thin, with the words *Equipages de ligne* engraved on it. That sort of button, I believe, went out with the last of the French Bourbons. "I preserved it from the time of my Navy Service," he explained, nodding rapidly his frail, vulture-like head. It was not very likely that he had picked up that relic in the street. He looked certainly old enough to have fought at Trafalgar—or, at any rate, to have played his little part there as a powder monkey. Shortly after we had been introduced he had informed me in a Franco-Provençal jargon, mumbling tremulously with his toothless jaws, that when he was a "shaver no higher than that" he had seen the Emperor Napoleon returning from Elba. It was at night, he narrated vaguely, without animation, at a spot between Frejus and Antibes in the open country. A big fire had been lit at the side of the cross-roads. The population from several villages had collected there, old and young—down to the very children in arms because the women had refused to stay at home. Tall soldiers, wearing high, hairy caps, stood in a circle facing the people silently, and their stern eyes and big mustaches were enough to make everybody keep at a distance. He, "being an impudent little shaver," wriggled out of the crowd, creeping on his hands and knees as near as he dared to the grenadiers' legs, and peeping through discovered, standing perfectly still in the light of the fire, "a little fat fellow in a three-cornered hat, buttoned up in a long straight coat, with a big, pale face, inclined on one shoulder, looking something like a priest. His hands were clasped behind his back . . . It appears that this was the Emperor," the Ancient commented with a faint sigh. He was staring from the ground with all his might, when "my poor father," who had been searching for his boy frantically every where, pounced upon him and hauled him away by the ear.

The tale seems an authentic recollection. He related it to me many times, using the very same words. The grandfather honoured me by a special and somewhat embarrassing predilection. Extremes touch. He was the oldest member by a long way in that Company, and I was, if I may say so, its temporarily adopted baby. He had been a pilot longer than any man in the boat could remember; thirty–forty years. He did not seem certain himself, but it could be found out, he suggested, in the archives of the Pilot Office. He had been pensioned off years before, but he went out from force of habit; and, as my friend the *patron* of the Company once confided to me in a whisper, "the old chap did no harm. He was not in the way." They treated him with rough deference. One and another would address some insignificant remark to him now and again, but nobody really took any notice of what he had to say. He had survived his strength, his usefulness, his very wisdom. He wore long, green, worsted stockings, pulled up above the knee over his trousers, a sort of woollen nightcap on his hairless cranium, and wooden clogs on his feet. Without his hooded cloak he looked like a peasant. Half a dozen hands would be extended to help him on board, but afterward he was left pretty much to his own thoughts. Of course he never did any work, except, perhaps, to cast off some rope when hailed, "*Hé, l'Ancien!* let go the halyards there, at your hand"—or some such request of an easy kind.

No one took notice in any way of the chuckling within the shadow of the hood. He kept it up for a long time with intense enjoyment. Obviously he had preserved intact the innocence of mind which is easily amused. But when his hilarity had exhausted itself, he made a professional remark in a self-assertive but quavering voice:

"Can't expect much work on a night like this."

No one took it up. It was a mere truism. Nothing under canvas could be expected to make a port on such an idle night of dreamy splendour and spiritual stillness. We would have to glide idly to and fro, keeping our station within the appointed bearings, and, unless a fresh breeze sprang up with the dawn, we would land before sunrise on a small islet that, within two miles of us, shone like a lump of frozen moonlight, to "break a crust and take a pull at the wine bottle." I was familiar with the procedure. The stout boat emptied of her crowd would nestle her buoyant, capable side against the very rock—such is the perfectly smooth amenity of the classic sea when in a gentle mood. The crust broken and the mouthful of wine swallowed—it was literally no more than that with this abstemious race—the pilots would pass the time stamping their feet on the slabs of sea-salted stone and blowing into their nipped fingers. One or two misanthropists would sit apart, perched on boulders like man-like sea-fowl of solitary habits; the sociably disposed would gossip scandalously in little gesticulating knots; and there would be perpetually one or another of my hosts taking aim at the empty horizon with the long, brass tube of the telescope, a heavy, murderous-looking piece of collective property, everlastingly changing hands with brandishing and levelling movements. Then about noon (it was a short turn of duty—the long turn lasted twenty-four hours) another boatful of pilots would relieve us—and we should steer for the old Phœnician port, dominated, watched over from the ridge of a dust-grey, arid hill by the red-and-white striped pile of the Notre Dame de la Garde.

All this came to pass as I had foreseen in the fullness of my very recent experience. But also something not foreseen by me did happen, something which causes me to remember my last outing with the pilots. It was on this occasion that my hand touched, for the first time, the side of an English ship.

No fresh breeze had come with the dawn, only the steady little draught got a more keen edge on it as the eastern sky became bright and glassy with a clean, colourless light. It was while we were all ashore on the islet that a steamer was picked up by the telescope, a black speck like an insect posed on the hard edge of the offing. She emerged rapidly to her water-line and came on steadily, a slim hull with a long streak of smoke slanting away from the rising sun. We embarked in a hurry, and headed the boat out for our prey, but we hardly moved three miles an hour.

She was a big, high-class cargo-steamer of a type that is to be met on the sea no more, black hull, with low, white super-structures, powerfully rigged with three masts and a lot of yards on the fore; two hands at her enormous wheel—steam steering-gear was not a matter of course in these days—and with them on the bridge three others, bulky in thick blue jackets, ruddy-faced, muffled up, with peaked caps—I suppose all her officers. There are ships I have met more than once and known well by sight whose names I have forgotten; but the name of that ship seen once so many years ago in the clear flush of a cold, pale sunrise I have not forgotten. How could I—the first English ship on whose side I ever laid my hand! The name—I read it letter by letter on the bow—was *James Westoll*. Not very romantic, you will say. The name of a very considerable, well-known, and universally respected North-country shipowner, I believe. James Westoll! What better name could an honourable hard-working ship have? To me the very grouping of the letters is alive with the romantic feeling of her reality as I saw her floating motionless and borrowing an ideal grace from the austere purity of the light.

We were then very near her and, on a sudden impulse, I volunteered to pull bow in the dinghy which shoved off at once to put the pilot on board while our boat, fanned by the faint air which had attended us all through the night, went on gliding gently past the black, glistening length of the ship. A few strokes brought us alongside, and it was then that, for the very first time in my life, I heard myself addressed in English—the speech of my secret choice, of my future, of long friendships, of the deepest affections, of hours of toil and hours of ease, and of solitary hours, too, of books read, of thoughts pursued, of remembered emotions—of my very dreams! And if (after being thus fashioned by it in that part of me which cannot decay) I dare not claim it aloud as my own, then, at any rate, the speech of my children. Thus small events grow memorable by the passage of time. As to the quality of the address itself I cannot say it was very striking. Too short for eloquence and devoid of all charm of tone, it consisted precisely of the three words "Look out there!" growled out huskily above my head.

It proceeded from a big fat fellow—he had an obtrusive, hairy double chin—in a blue woollen shirt and roomy breeches pulled up very high, even to the level of his breastbone, by a pair of braces quite exposed to public view. As where he stood there was no bulwark, but only a rail and stanchions, I was able to take in at a glance the whole of his voluminous person from his feet to the high crown of his soft black hat, which sat like an absurd flanged cone on his big head. The grotesque and massive aspect of that deck hand (I suppose he was that—very likely the lamp-trimmer) surprised me very much. My course of reading, of dreaming and longing for the sea had not prepared me for a sea-brother of that sort. I never met again a figure in the least like his except in the illustrations to Mr. W.W. Jacobs' most entertaining tales of barges and coasters; but the inspired talent of Mr. Jacobs for poking endless fun at poor, innocent sailors in a prose which, however extravagant in its felicitous invention, is always artistically adjusted to observed truth, was not yet. Perhaps Mr. Jacobs himself was not yet. I fancy that, at most, if he had made his nurse laugh it was about all he had achieved at that early date.

Therefore, I repeat, other disabilities apart, I could not have been prepared for the sight of that husky old porpoise. The object of his concise address was to call my attention to a rope which he incontinently flung down for me to catch. I caught it, though it was not really necessary, the ship having no way on her by that time. Then everything went on very swiftly. The dinghy came with a slight bump against the steamer's side, the pilot, grabbing for the rope ladder, had scrambled half-way up before I knew that our task of boarding was done; the harsh, muffled clanging of the engine-room telegraph struck my ear through the iron plate; my companion in the dinghy was urging me to "shove off—push hard"; and when I bore against the smooth flank of the first English ship I ever touched in my life, I felt it already throbbing under my open palm.

Her head swung a little to the west, pointing toward the miniature lighthouse of the Jolliette breakwater, far away there, hardly distinguishable against the land. The dinghy danced a squashy, splashy jig in the wash of the wake and turning in my seat I followed the *James Westoll* with my eyes. Before she had gone in a quarter of a mile she hoisted her flag, as the harbour regulations prescribe for arriving and departing ships. I saw it suddenly flicker and stream out on the flag staff. The Red Ensign! In the pellucid, colourless atmosphere bathing the drab and grey masses of that southern land, the livid islets, the sea of pale glassy blue under the pale glassy sky of that cold sunrise, it was, as far as the eye could reach, the only spot of ardent colour—flamelike, intense, and presently as minute as the tiny red spark the concentrated reflection of a great fire kindles in the clear heart of a globe of crystal. The Red Ensign—the symbolic, protecting, warm bit of bunting flung wide upon the seas, and destined for so many years to be the only roof over my head.

THE SEA GHOST

EDMUND BLUNDEN

Poet, novelist, and essayist Edmund Blunden (1896–1974) was born in Sussex, England. He joined the Royal Sussex Regiment in 1916 and fought almost continuously at the front lines in France during the First World War, an experience he later recounted in *Undertones of War* (1928). A friend of Siegfried Sassoon and Robert Graves, he was recognized as one of the foremost war poets of his generation. In 1924, and off and on for the next twenty years, he taught at the University of Tokyo; in 1931 he was also made a fellow of Merton College, Oxford, where one of his students was the future Canadian literary critic Northrop Frye. Suffering from what would today be called post-traumatic stress disorder after his war service, Blunden sailed to Argentina as a rest cure. His account of that cruise, *The Bonadventure: A Random Journal of an Atlantic Holiday,* was published in 1922, and it is from that lively and endearing record that the following excerpt has been taken.

IT BLEW FROM the north-east strong against us always, and we were travelling more slowly. The sun returned, however, among those ethereal white clouds which to perfection fulfil the poet's word "Pavilions"; we ran on into a dark sea ridged and rilled with glintering silver, yet seemed never to reach it, remaining in a bright blue race of waters scattered, port and starboard, with white wreaths, waters leaping from the heavy flanks of the ship in a seethe of gossamer atoms and glass-green cascade.

The immediate scene was one of painters and paint-pots, and linen flying on the lines. "This wind's playing hell with my curls," said one or two. The matter with me was, that my room was almost untenable. I opened the port at my peril; to do so was to entertain billows of coal-dust from the bunkers below. White paint, the order of the day, whether flat white or white enamel, made progress about the ship by an amateur dangerous, too.

The apparition of the steward under the evening lamps dressed in a smock—he was of ample make—and brandishing a paint-brush, was generally enjoyed. In fact, several spectators came to take a careful look at one who was too often denomi-nated "the mouldy-headed old ——."

A more tenuous apparition was heard of, as we ran north. Whether a hoax or not, I do not know. My first information of it came in the form of a drawing by the apprentice Tich, showing the ship's bell being struck by a hand who never was on land or sea, and apprentice Lamb leaving his hold of the wheel in horror, and even Mead shaking all over and gaping. A poem appended said that the facts were what the picture made out. The *Bonad-venture* was so new a ship—her old name, showing her war origin, still stood on the bells and the blue prints in the chartroom and elsewhere—that there seemed every likelihood against the story being the truth. I asked Mead, and he told me what he maintained to be true.

On the first watch, the voyage before this, he had gone into the wheel-house for a word with the apprentice at the wheel. A shadow, indistinct, yet leaving impressed on his recollection a human shape, slipped suddenly past the wheel-house windows, softly rang the bell once, and swiftly departed. The frightened boy drops the wheel, lets the ship swing round completely out of her course: Mead runs out, but there is nothing to be seen. He sends for the two A.B.'s who might have come up on the bridge, but they say that they have not done so, nor indeed would they come without object. The firemen, if they have to communicate with the bridge, never come higher than the stairway to the bridge deck, and it proved that no one of them had been there. By the wheel-house clock, it was noticed that the precise time of the visitation was 10:15, an hour not hitherto regarded by ghosts, I believe, as preferable to midnight.

And more. Still imagining that some practical joker was at work, Mead brought a big stick with him on his watch. This was no remedy. The ghost appeared again, at much the same hour, on several nights; it was remarked, mostly when the apprentice who first saw it had the wheel. Trying to stop so strange a bell-ringer, Mead was met by a sharp flap of wind, from a dead still night, and the glimmering shadow was gone to the air. All this happened north of the line.

This was Mead's story, but the boy's seemed to support it; and when in the shadows of the bridge deck, earnestly and without trimming, he told it me, it seemed very true. I glanced about me occasionally after hearing it.

The wind continued, but the heat was becoming intense. Painting went on like the wind. The derricks received a terra-cotta coat and their trellis work looked an amenity, against the general whiteness. The fervour for redecoration even affected me: was not my hutch to share the common lot? But, though the walls needed it, the matter was postponed, on account of the limited accommodation.

The newspaper was to appear again, but its circulation was being cut down. One copy only would now have to serve the public. It was passed to me, and my aid with paragraphs requested. I could not regret the reduction made in the number, even though if that one copy was lost,

We knew not where was that Promethean torch
That could its light relumine.

Bicker, the editor, instead of reviewing his admired literature in his journal, lengthened breakfast by doing so there *viva voce*. He was all for Bœotian situations, and, on occasion, his cold re-dishing was tactfully ended by a relief conversation on religion, the keynote of which was in the unironically meant remark: "He was darned religious, but he was a darned good man." I began to know a certain captain, from talk during the voyage, almost by sight; one who "went in for Sunday Schools, and put on a crown of glory as soon as he reached Wales," but once away again, it appears that "he fell."

Another matter for the columns of the *Optimist* was obtruded upon the breakfast table. It was a conundrum:

West was the wind, and West steered we,
West was the land. How could that be?

The answer, apart from such evasions as "You were entering port," was that West was the name of the helmsman. It was understood that the poem went on in this strain, but the chief's protest came in time.

The cat (last heard of in disgrace), which was under the especial care of the mess-room boy, was no doubt pleased hereabouts by our reaching the regions of flying-fishes; but nevertheless continued, on the gospel of Kelly, to take a chair in the engineer's mess at the critical hours of twelve and five. I myself saw her there at twelve once or twice, judging the time, no doubt, by the parade of table-cloth and cutlery.

Without any abatement of the stuffy heat inside our cabins, we ran into a rainy area. The sea was overcast, and the showers splashed us well. Meanwhile, the wind had veered round more to the east, and besides bringing the grey vapours of rain tumultuously towards us thence, set the spray flying over the lower decks and kept us on the roll. Blowing on the beam, however, it seemed to please Phillips, ever anxious about the hourly ten knots which seemed too high an expectation. Squalls threatened; it was a tropical April mood. The rolling influenced my sleep, in which I fancied myself manipulating the airiest pleasure-boats, overcrowded with passengers who refused to sit down, on an angry flooded river.

The peaceful disposition of the four apprentices began to weigh upon Mead's mind. A very happy and orderly set they were, although the current *Optimist* contained an illustrated article on the bosun's tyrannie, as:

"Youse take them two derricks for'ard."

"Youse jes' pick up that ventilator, you flat-nosed son of a sea-cook."

The drawings of the well-known walrus head under the antique, unique grey (*né* white) one-sided sugar-loaf hat, were admirable. But to proceed. The four boys were of the best behaviour, occasionally, indeed, laughing or playing mouth-organs at unpopular hours, or even after the nightly exit of the cook making flap-jacks, otherwise pancakes, from his properties in the galley. When I joined Mead on his watch, one Sunday evening, he began to "wonder what the boys are coming to." They were not like the boys of his time. He delved into his own apprentice autobiography, and rediscovered an era, a blissful era of whirling fists, blood, and booby traps.

A day followed remarkable for the weather. A swell caused the ship to roll with a will all day, but, as was expected in the doldrums, the wind slackened. After a few hours of this lull, there was a piping and groaning through all the scanty rigging that the steamer owned, and from farther out to sea the grey obscurity of violent rain-storm, much as it had done on our way south, bore down upon us. Soon the ship was cloaked close in a cloud of rain pale as snow, which flecked the icy-looking sea, veined white alongside us, with dark speckling bubbles. Then it was time to sound the whistle, and its doleful groan went out again and again (the wind still varying its note from a drone to a howl) until the fiercer sting of the rain was spent, and distance began to grow ahead of the ship. This storm lacked thunder and lightning; and yet, when Sparks invited me to listen to his "lovely X-s," there was a continuous and furious rolling uproar in the phones. Then, as strange again, as if at a nod that din came to a sudden stop, leaving in the phones a lucid calm in which ship-signals rang out clear.

At sunset of a day which washed off the new paint as soon as (in the intervals) it had been put on, a thin red fringe glowed along the horizon, making me long for green hills and white spires; at night, the stars from Southern Cross to Charles's Waggon were gleaming, but the sea lay profoundly black, and upon it all round us came and went glory after glory of water-fire. The next day, however, it rained in the same dismal style, and the sun's eclipse and the passing of Fernando Noronha were but little heeded. I was called a Jonah by every one.

A mollyhawk, that evening, created some excitement. He first spent some time in flying on an oval course round the ship, for his recreation, it looked. His beautiful curves must have pleased him as they did me, for he persuaded (or so it appeared) another mollyhawk to make the circuit with him. Meacock and myself heard one of these strike against the wireless aerial, and thought that it would have scared them away; but no, a few minutes later we heard a croaking and a flapping while we stood in the lee of the wheel-house, and there was a mollyhawk. He had struck some low rope or fixture. He was prevented by his webbed feet from rising again, and I had fears for his future, which were by no means necessary; for Meacock followed him, an awkward but speedy walker, down to the lower bridge deck, and, fearing the swift white stabbing bill, waiting his chance, suddenly caught at his nearest wing and launched him into the air. If his speed could show it, that bird was relieved.

This incident was a welcome verification of some of the saloon's bird anecdotes; and though it was nearly dark and the bird was only aboard for two or three minutes, his release was watched by a very good gathering, representative of engineers, firemen, the galley, sailors, and apprentices.

A PACIFIC TRAVERSE

JACK LONDON

Jack London (1876–1916) was born in San Francisco, signed onto a sealing vessel at the age of seventeen, and visited Japan and the Arctic. He joined the Klondike gold rush in 1897 and, although he didn't strike a bonanza in gold, later turned that experience into extremely lucrative fiction. *The Son of the Wolf* (1900) and *A Daughter of the Snows* (1902) were both set in the Klondike, and his first major success, *The Call of the Wild* (1903), was set in Alaska. London designed the *Snark,* a forty-five-foot ketch, to realize a boyhood dream of sailing the Pacific. With his second wife, Charmian Kittredge, he and a small crew left San Francisco in April 1907 for Hawaii, travelling through the South Seas before arriving in Australia in November 1908. The following passage, describing a sixty-day calm in "the variables" above the equator, is taken from London's account of the voyage, *The Cruise of the Snark* (1911).

· · ·

IT LOOKED EASY on paper. Here was Hilo and there was our objective, 128° west longitude. With the northeast trade blowing we could travel a straight line between the two points, and even slack our sheets off a goodly bit. But one of the chief troubles with the trades is that one never knows just where he will pick them up and just in what direction they will be blowing. We picked up the northeast trade right outside of Hilo harbour, but the miserable breeze was away around into the east. Then there was the north equatorial current setting westward like a mighty river. Furthermore, a small boat, by the wind and bucking into a big headsea, does not work to advantage. She jogs up and down and gets nowhere. Her sails are full and straining, every little while she presses her lee-rail under, she flounders, and bumps, and splashes, and that is all. Whenever she begins to gather way, she runs ker-chug into a big mountain of water and is brought to a standstill. So, with the *Snark,* the resultant of her smallness, of the trade around into the east, and of the strong equatorial current, was a long sag south. Oh, she did not go quite south. But the easting she made was distressing. On October 11, she made forty miles easting; October 12, fifteen miles; October 13, no easting; October 14, thirty miles; October 15, twenty-three miles; October 16, eleven miles; and on October 17, she actually went to the westward four miles. Thus, in a week she made one hundred and fifteen miles easting, which was equivalent to sixteen miles a day. But, between the longitude of Hilo and 128 ° west longitude is a difference of twenty-seven degrees, or, roughly, sixteen hundred miles. At sixteen miles a day, one hundred days would be required to accomplish this distance. And even then, our objective, 128° west longitude, was five degrees north of the Line, while Nuka-hiva, in the Marquesas, lay nine degrees south of the Line and twelve degrees to the west!

There remained only one thing to do—to work south out of the trade and into the variables. It is true that Captain Bruce found no variables on his traverse, and that he "never could make easting on either tack." It was the variables or nothing with us, and we prayed for better luck than he had had. The variables constitute the belt of ocean lying between the trades and the doldrums, and are conjectured to be the draughts of heated air which rise in the doldrums, flow high in the air counter to the trades, and gradually sink down till they fan the surface of the ocean where they are found. And they are found . . . where they are found; for they are wedged between the trades and the doldrums, which same shift their territory from day to day and month to month.

We found the variables in 11° north latitude, and 11° north latitude we hugged jealously. To the south lay the doldrums. To the north lay the northeast trade that refused to blow from the northeast. The days came and went, and always they found the *Snark* somewhere near the eleventh parallel. The variables were truly variable. A light head-wind would die away and leave us rolling in a calm for forty-eight hours. Then a light head-wind would spring up, blow for three hours, and leave us rolling in another calm for forty-eight hours. Then—hurrah!—the wind would come out of the west, fresh, beautifully fresh, and send the *Snark* along, wing and wing, her wake bubbling, the log-line straight astern. At the end of half an hour, while we were preparing to set the spinnaker, with a few sickly gasps the wind would die away. And so it went. We wagered optimistically on every favourable fan of air that lasted over five minutes; but it never did any good. The fans faded out just the same.

But there were exceptions. In the variables, if you wait long enough, something is bound to happen, and we were so plentifully stocked with food and water that we could afford to wait. On October 26, we actually made one hundred and three miles of easting, and we talked about it for days afterwards. Once we caught a moderate gale from the south, which blew itself out in eight hours, but it helped us to seventy-one miles of easting in that particular twenty-four hours. And then, just as it was expiring, the wind came straight out from the north (the directly opposite quarter), and fanned us along over another degree of easting.

In years and years no sailing vessel has attempted this traverse, and we found ourselves in the midst of one of the loneliest of the Pacific solitudes. In the sixty days we were crossing it we sighted no sail, lifted no steamer's smoke above the horizon. A disabled vessel could drift in this deserted expanse for a dozen generations, and there would be no rescue. The only chance of rescue would be from a vessel like the *Snark,* and the *Snark* happened to be there principally because of the fact that the traverse had been begun before the particular paragraph in the sailing directions had been read. Standing upright on deck, a straight line drawn from the eye to the horizon would measure three miles and a half. Thus, seven miles was the diameter of the circle of the sea in which we had our centre. Since we remained always in the centre, and since we constantly were moving in some direction, we looked upon many circles. But all circles looked alike. No tufted islets, gray headlands, nor glistening patches of white canvas ever marred the symmetry of that unbroken curve. Clouds came and went, rising up over the rim of the circle, flowing across the space of it, and spilling away and down across the opposite rim. The world faded as the procession of the weeks marched by. The world faded until at last there ceased to be any world except the little world of the *Snark*, freighted with her seven souls and floating on the expanse of the waters. Our memories of the world, the great world, became like dreams of former lives we had lived somewhere before we came to be born on the *Snark*. After we had been out of fresh vegetables for some time, we mentioned such things in much the same way I have heard my father mention the vanished apples of his boyhood. Man is a creature of habit, and we on the *Snark* had got the habit of the *Snark*. Everything about her and aboard her was as a matter of course, and anything different would have been an irritation and an offence.

There was no way by which the great world could intrude. Our bell rang the hours, but no caller ever rang it. There were no guests to dinner, no telegrams, no insistent telephone jangles invading our privacy. We had no engagements to keep, no trains to catch, and there were no morning newspapers over which to waste time in learning what was happening to our fifteen hundred million other fellow-creatures.

But it was not dull. The affairs of our little world had to be regulated, and, unlike the great world, our world had to be steered in its journey through space. Also, there were cosmic disturbances to be encountered and baffled, such as do not afflict the big earth in its frictionless orbit through the windless void. And we never knew, from moment to moment, what was going to happen next. There were spice and variety enough and to spare. Thus, at four in the morning, I relieve Hermann at the wheel.

"East-northeast," he gives me the course. "She's eight points off, but she ain't steering."

Small wonder. The vessel does not exist that can be steered in so absolute a calm.

"I had a breeze a little while ago—maybe it will come back again," Hermann says hopefully, ere he starts forward to the cabin and his bunk.

The mizzen is in and fast furled. In the night, what of the roll and the absence of wind, it had made life too hideous to be permitted to go on rasping at the mast, smashing at the tackles, and buffeting the empty air into hollow outbursts of sound. But the big mainsail is still on, and the staysail, jib, and flying-jib are snapping and slashing at their sheets with every roll. Every star is out. Just for luck I put the wheel hard over in the opposite direction to which it had been left by Hermann, and I lean back and gaze up at the stars. There is nothing else for me to do. There is nothing to be done with a sailing vessel rolling in a stark calm.

Then I feel a fan on my cheek, faint, so faint, that I can just sense it ere it is gone. But another comes, and another, until a real and just perceptible breeze is blowing. How the *Snark*'s sails manage to feel it is beyond me, but feel it they do, as she does as well, for the compass card begins slowly to revolve in the binnacle. In reality, it is not revolving at all. It is held by terrestrial magnetism in one place, and it is the *Snark* that is revolving, pivoted upon that delicate cardboard device that floats in a closed vessel of alcohol.

So the *Snark* comes back on her course. The breath increases to a tiny puff. The *Snark* feels the weight of it and actually heels over a trifle. There is flying scud overhead, and I notice the stars being blotted out. Walls of darkness close in upon me, so that, when the last star is gone, the darkness is so near that it seems I can reach out and touch it on every side. When I lean toward it, I can feel it loom against my face. Puff follows puff, and I am glad the mizzen is furled. Phew! that was a stiff one! The *Snark* goes over and down until her lee-rail is buried and the whole Pacific Ocean is pouring in. Four or five of these gusts make me wish that the jib and flying-jib were in. The sea is picking up, the gusts are growing stronger and more frequent, and there is a splatter of wet in the air. There is no use in attempting to gaze to windward. The wall of blackness is within arm's length. Yet I cannot help attempting to see and gauge the blows that are being struck at the *Snark*. There is something ominous and menacing up there to windward, and I have a feeling that if I look long enough and strong enough, I shall divine it. Futile feeling. Between two gusts I leave the wheel and run forward to the cabin companionway, where I light matches and consult the barometer. "29–90" it reads. That sensitive instrument refuses to take notice of the disturbance which is humming with a deep, throaty voice in the rigging. I get back to the wheel just in time to meet another gust, the strongest yet. Well, anyway, the wind is abeam and the *Snark* is on her course, eating up easting. That at least is well.

The jib and flying-jib bother me, and I wish they were in. She would make easier weather of it, and less risky weather likewise. The wind snorts, and stray raindrops pelt like birdshot. I shall certainly have to call all hands, I conclude; then conclude the next instant to hang on a little longer. Maybe this is the end of it, and I shall have called them for nothing. It is better to let them sleep. I hold the *Snark* down to her task, and from out of the darkness, at right angles, comes a deluge of rain accompanied by shrieking wind. Then everything eases except the blackness, and I rejoice in that I have not called the men.

No sooner does the wind ease than the sea picks up. The combers are breaking now, and the boat is tossing like a cork. Then out of the blackness the gusts come harder and faster than before. If only I knew what was up there to windward in the blackness! The *Snark* is making heavy weather of it, and her lee-rail is buried oftener than not. More shrieks and snorts of wind. Now, if ever, is the time to call the men. I *will* call them, I resolve. Then there is a burst of rain, a slackening of the wind, and I do not call. But it is rather lonely, there at the wheel, steering a little world through howling blackness. It is quite a responsibility to be all alone on the surface of a little world in time of stress, doing the thinking for its sleeping inhabitants. I recoil from the responsibility as more gusts begin to strike and as a sea licks along the weather rail and splashes over into the cockpit. The salt water seems strangely warm to my body and is shot through with ghostly nodules of phosphorescent light. I shall surely call all hands to shorten sail. Why should they sleep? I am a fool to have any compunctions in the matter. My intellect is arrayed against my heart. It was my heart that said, "Let them sleep." Yes, but it was my intellect that backed up my heart in that judgment. Let my intellect then reverse the judgment; and, while I am speculating as to what particular entity issued that command to my intellect, the gusts die away. Solicitude for mere bodily comfort has no place in practical seamanship, I conclude sagely; but study the feel of the next series of gusts and do not call the men. After all, it *is* my intellect, behind everything, procrastinating, measuring its knowledge of what the *Snark* can endure against the blows being struck at her, and waiting the call of all hands against the striking of still severer blows.

Daylight, gray and violent, steals through the cloud-pall and shows a foaming sea that flattens under the weight of recurrent and increasing squalls. Then comes the rain, filling the windy valleys of the sea with milky smoke and further flattening the waves, which but wait for the easement of wind and rain to leap more wildly than before. Come the men on deck, their sleep out, and among them Hermann, on his face the broad grin in appreciation of the breeze of wind I have picked up. I turn the wheel over to Warren and start to go below, pausing on the way to rescue the galley stovepipe which has gone adrift. I am bare-footed, and my toes have had an excellent education in the art of clinging; but, as the rail buries itself in a green sea, I suddenly sit down on the streaming deck. Hermann good-naturedly elects to question my selection of such a spot. Then comes the next roll, and he sits down, suddenly, and without premeditation. The *Snark* heels over and down, the rail takes it green, and Her-mann and I, clutching the precious stove-pipe, are swept down into the lee-scuppers. After that I finish my journey below, and while changing my clothes grin with satisfaction—the *Snark* is making easting.

LAT. 63° 56′ 40″ N.
LONG. 51° 19′ 00″ W.

ROCKWELL KENT

O ne of the most celebrated landscape painters of the last century,
Rockwell Kent was born in Tarrytown Heights, New York, in 1882.
After studying architecture at Columbia University, he moved to Monhe-
gan Island, Maine, in 1905, where he mastered the art of the seascape. He
moved to Brigus, Newfoundland, in 1914, but was deported the following
year under suspicion of being a German spy. (Michael Winter's 2004 novel
The Big Why is based on Kent's Newfoundland experience.) Thereafter, he
lived on Fox Island, Alaska, and Tierra del Fuego, and, in 1929, decided to
sail to Greenland. This excerpt from his book about that voyage, *N by E*
(1930), describes the shipwreck that ended the adventure but did not blunt
Kent's love of the rugged Greenland coastline. His famous illustrated edi-
tion of *Moby Dick* also appeared in 1930 and helped restore that novel to
its status as an American classic. Kent wrote his autobiography, *It's Me, O
Lord*, in 1955, and died in the Adirondacks in 1971.

THE MOTION WOKE me. Where was I? I remembered. Daylight came but faintly through the fo'castle ports, shadowed as they were by the dinghy. My clock showed ten-thirty. How I had slept!

We were rolling violently; a sudden roll, a lurch to starboard. I heard steps on deck, voices, the sound of hawser paying out. Oh, well, we're at anchor; and no one has called. I braced my knees against the side board of the bunk; I had need to.

Suddenly we were careened so far that I was almost catapulted onto the floor. I got out, dressed hastily and opened the door into the cabin. It was broad daylight there. The skipper was in bed.

"She's drifting with both anchors," called the mate from the deck.

"Give 'em more rope," answered the skipper.

I reached the ladder. At that moment, something rolled us over, far, far down, and held us there; and the green sea came pouring in as if to fill the ship.

"Damn it!" I cried. "And I'd made everything so neat!"

On deck a hurricane; I'd never felt such wind before. The sea was beaten flat, with every wave crest shorn and whipped to smoke; cold spray and stinging wind drove over us.

I helped the mate. "We'll need the third anchor," I said, and started aft.

The skipper appeared. "Good, get it out," he said as I passed him. I went below for the last time.

The spare anchor was knocked down and stowed under the coal sacks and provisions in the after hold; it was not easy to come at. Removing the companion ladder I set to work. Hard work it was, cramped in that narrow space on hands and knees. As I dragged the hundred pound sacks out onto the cabin floor—always, strangely, careful not to damage anything—I'd look up and see the gray sky through the opening above my head. Then one time glancing up I saw the brow of the mountain; and always after that more mountain showed and less sky. And at last the mountainside itself seemed to have moved against the ship and to be towering over it.

I had laid a lighted cigarette carefully upon the chart table; this, as I worked, was always in my mind—that it should not be left to burn the wood. And so, from time to time, I'd move it just a bit. We were so careful of our boat, to mar it in no way!

But all the while I had been shifting goods and moving sacks of coal; so that at last I came to the anchor. It was a large anchor and very heavy. I dragged it out into the cabin.

"Come," I called to the mate, "and help me get this thing on deck." And as I looked up I saw the mate in his yellow oilskins, bright against the near dark mountainside.

"Not much use now," said the mate; but he came down.

It was hard work to lift that anchor up, and we seemed not to be very strong. "I lose my strength from excitement," said the mate. I thought that I did too—but didn't say so.

We lifted the cumbersome affair head high and tumbled it out into the cockpit. As I started to follow, a great sea lifted us and rolled us over; I hung on, half out of the cabin. And I stared straight at an oncoming wall or rock so near astern it seemed about to crush us. The sea rose high against it, and broke and became churned water that seethed around us. It cradled us and lowered us gently; and the dark land drew quietly away.

Then came another sea that hurled us and the land together. "Now for the crash!" I thought—and I gripped hard and braced myself against it, and watched the moment—thrilled by its impending horror.

There was no crash—that time. Ever so gently, just as we seemed to draw away again, our stern post touched the ledge; so lightly touched that it made no sound, only a little tremor. And the tremor ran through the iron keel and the oak, and through the ribs and planking, and through every bolt and nail, through every fibre of the boat and us. Maybe we had not known that the end had come; now, as if God whispered it, we knew.

So for a third time we were floated back.

Then, as if the furies of the sea and wind were freed at last to end their coquetry, they lifted us—high, high above the ledge—and dropped us there. And the impact of that shock was only less than those that followed for that half an hour until *Direction* sank.

That half an hour! We lay, caught in the angle of a giant step of rock, keel on the tread and starboard side against the riser; held there by wind and sea; held there to lift and pound; to lift so buoyantly on every wave; to drop—crashing our thirteen iron-shod tons on granite. Lift and pound! There the perfection of our ship revealed itself; only, that having stuck just once, she ever lived, a ship, to lift and strike again.

A giant sledge hammer striking a granite mountain; a hollow

hammer; and within it a man. Picture yourself the man. I stayed below, and was.

See me as Adam; set full blown into that pandemonium of force, his world—of wind, storm, snow, rain, hail, lightning and thunder, earthquake and flood, hunger and cold, and the huge terrifying presence of the unknown—using his little wit toward self containedness against the too-much of immensity; and quietly—for Adam lived—doing the little first-at-hands one on another in their natural course, thinking but little and reflecting less. Adam and Man; and me in that compacted miniature of man's universe, the cabin of the yacht *Direction* on the rocks of Greenland.

We live less by imagination than despite it.

THE ICEBERG

E. J. PRATT

Edwin John Pratt (1882–1964) was born in Newfoundland, the son of a Methodist minister who moved from outport to outport. Pratt himself became a preacher and missionary while attending Victoria College, University of Toronto, and earned a doctorate in theology. From 1920 until 1953, he taught in the English department at Victoria College, during which time he became one of Canada's major poets. His first collection, *Newfoundland Verse*, appeared in 1923 and set out Pratt's lifelong preoccupation with the sea as both provider and destroyer. The theme is continued in "The Titanic" (1935), which pits humankind against Nature (with Nature winning, of course) and mocks the hubris of man's assurance that he has built an unsinkable ship. The following excerpt describes—even personifies—the iceberg that eventually fulfills the *Titanic*'s tragic destiny.

. . .

Calved from a glacier near Godhaven coast,
It left the fiord for the sea—a host
Of white flotillas gathering in its wake,

And joined by fragments from a Behring floe,
Had circumnavigated it to make
It centre of an archipelago,
Its lateral motion on the Davis Strait
Was casual and indeterminate,
And each advance to southward was as blind
As each recession to the north. No smoke
Of steamships nor the hoist of mainsails broke
The polar wastes—no sounds except the grind
Of ice, the cry of curlews and the lore
Of winds from mesas of eternal snow;
Until caught by the western undertow,
It struck the current of the Labrador
Which swung it to its definite southern stride.
Pressure and glacial time had stratified
The berg to the consistency of flint,
And kept inviolate, through clash of tide
And gale, façade and columns with their hint
Of inward altars and of steepled bells
Ringing the passage of the parallels.
But when with months of voyaging it came
To where both streams—the Gulf and Polar—met,
The sun which left its crystal peaks aflame
In the sub-arctic noons, began to fret
The arches, flute the spires and deform
The features, till the batteries of storm,
Playing above the slow-eroding base,

Demolished the last temple touch of grace.
Another month, and nothing but the brute
And palaeolithic outline of a face
Fronted the transatlantic shipping route.
A sloping spur that tapered to a claw
And lying twenty feet below had made
It lurch and shamble like a plantigrade;
But with an impulse governed by the raw
Mechanics of its birth, it drifted where
Ambushed, fog-gray, it stumbled on its lair,
North forty-one degrees and forty-four,
Fifty and fourteen west the longitude,
Waiting a world-memorial hour, its rude
Corundum form stripped to its Greenland core.

THE ARAFURA SEA

In 1932, Australian writer Dora Birtles (1904–1996) and five inexperienced companions set out from Newcastle, Australia, to sail around the world in a thirty-four-foot, motorless sailing ship called the *Skaga*, more or less on a whim. The expedition lasted less than a year, but they travelled five thousand miles, ending up in Makassar, East Indonesia, after a series of hardships recounted in Birtles's frank book, *Northwest by North*. Published in 1935, it is, in Birtles's words, "A Dante's *Inferno* description of maritime dyspepsia with no discomfort concealed." This passage describes a fierce storm the author experienced on a remote stretch of ocean between Merauke, New Guinea, and Dobo, a small island off the west coast of Tanahbesar Island, north of Australia.

. . .

ON THE MORNING of our departure from Merauke I had determined to get thin by fasting, so I had no breakfast and a dose of salts. However, after we got outside the weather became rough, the wind whistled cheerlessly, and it was cold and rainy. Smashing steep seas began to come up. We reefed the mainsail and I decided that it might be a good thing to postpone a fasting experiment till normal times. So I hastily mixed and drank some powdered milk and ate a large piece of indigestible currant bun. By the time for the midday meal it was very rough. The two girls were tucked in their bunks. A fortnight ashore had ruined their sea stomachs. Before we had left the harbour Ruth had thrown all manner of left-overs together into a large stew. Unfortunately it was awash with tinned tomatoes which in a juicy state I disliked, and the violet motion of the boat slopped the variegated stew out of the saucepan all over the tank top. My portion included a large weevil that ordinarily I might have disregarded, but now it was in the nature of the last straw. However, attracted by the warmth and in spite of my disapproval of the contents, I tried some and—was ignominiously sick.

So I laid low for awhile. The wind and the waves rose higher and Sven was ill! Sven, the sailor! Sven, who was never ill! Henery too confessed to qualms but he said his stomach refused to throw up. Sven and I blamed the stew, we had to blame something. That afternoon I had the five to eight PM watch and reflected gloomily that if I hadn't been so foolish as to change cookdays for Ruth's benefit the day before I might be snugly below instead of on deck in a racket of wind and rain.

Sunset was nothing but a smear of pale light between a green and foam-tossed sea and a cloud-covered sky. It was a dreadful watch. Our tiller was a large wooden handle, a heavy piece of timber without a block or tackle to get any mechanical advantage over the strain. All the weight of sea and wind coming against the keel was thrown directly against the steersman's strength. It was one continuous fight to keep her on her course. Sometimes the combing of the steering cockpit gave a little help. One could push the tiller over and then hold it jammed down against the combing for a few moments, not for long, because the worst blows came in shifting bursts, the wind had not steadied to a fixed direction or force. It leapt, violent and uncertain, at us. The waves too had their menace. They were steep and threatened to break on our deck and poop us. I remember being sick once or twice over the stern and holding on desperately to the kicking tiller, hoping nothing would happen during the crisis. Sven and Henery were making the gear tight for the night, consulting charts, filling lamps and coming up from time to time with anxious faces. The noise of the storm was a prolonged heavy sighing through the rigging. It did not seem loud until one had to shout against it to be heard.

Inside my right hand was a row of blisters. Even the calloused pads, result of long hours of steering, rose into blisters. The spray stung my eyes and dried out saltily on my face. The ends of my hair were little sodden flails whipping my cheeks. I could not push them back, both hands were gripped round the thick clumsy tiller under the sail-cloth cover we wore in bad weather. It made a tent over the steersman through which the water trickled. This was the worst time we had had since that first storm on the day of my leaving home. My arms and shoulders ached. I knew they would have to keep on aching, that nothing could be done about it. I hoped they would last out. The muscles of my back ached. I had to stand up and lean my weight shoving at that obstinate tiller to keep her over. There was no exultation in this storm, it was just a sea-sick misery. Fortunately the wind was favourable.

I recall plenty of heeling-over, water aboard, wind and obscurity but, outside the effort of my job, I cannot remember any detail of wave or wind in that watch. I do know that every moment of that interminable three hours crawled by and, when the end came, and there was still something Henery and Sven had to do and Sven asked, "Can you hang on a bit longer?" the bit longer felt an age, an unendurable extension of time. When at last he took over he had a flying gybe. The binnacle had not been lashed down and had fallen over in the welter, leaving him in complete darkness, and the course only allowed a narrow margin against jibing.

In my next watch, the dawn watch, the wind had settled. A sooty petrel, storm-caught, made a number of landings on the deck and finally lost its fear and settled below me in the galley, on top of the swinging gimbal, the nearest thing to a tree on board and the position of most stable equilibrium. At the time this odd occurrence roused no excitement in me. The bird and I after the first reconnoitring took no further interest in each other, we were fellow passengers brought together by necessity. A shrewd bird. He deserved to weather the storm. He only left about ten o'clock the next morning and he left in a hurry as a passenger leaves a train, without gratitude. In our first twenty-four hours out from Merauke we had done one hundred and thirty-seven miles, our best daily average for the trip.

There followed another stormy day of steady wind and heavy but not terrible steering. The crew was picking up and three of us eating well. Our main endeavour was to keep warm and dry.

On the third day it was still wet and windy and I woke with tonsils the size of pigeon's eggs. Between watches I slept and dozed, dreamt, and slept again in a mazed and invalidish confusion about time. My uneasy sleep was filled with unpleasant dreams, incoherent dreams of home and childhood so that I rose with joy to take the dog watch, as we had named the 1 AM to 3 AM watch. Ruth, whom I relieved, said, "Sit this side, keep the boom end in the track of the moon and she steers easily." So I sat staring at the moon which was a boat whose sail was invisible, continually passing ours in the opposite direction and never arriving. The sea was its usual midnight blue, a blue that was almost black. Big walls of water rose astern, *Skaga* would tilt up, lift high, shiver, and under us they passed. But I did not have to steady her down each separate slope as on that first agonizing night out.

Dog watch on the Arafura sea. It is strange how night, the moon and silence turn one's thoughts out. I had been thinking of childhood fantasies and of the mystery of birth. Watching it, as we rocked over its heaving waters, the sea became for me the All-Mother, the watery womb that produced the first life, the

moon, the eternal female. "Green-eyed women of the moon."
A Mother Carey's chicken or a petrel kept flying round and
round in circles over my head and over the wake stretched like
a galloping mare's tail behind the boat. The bird was so black
against the moon. I thought that had my dream desires been
fulfilled, I had read them as motherhood longings, it might be
a disembodied spirit trying to get a lodgment within me. That
conviction grew as the bird kept on weaving the rings of its
flight about me. Finally it perched near the end of the boom not
a yard from me. Its tail folded looked like a pair of scissors half-
open. It made no sound, its beak pointing as if it would pierce
my breast. Fascinated I let the ship get off the course a little and
was aware of a wave bigger than any that night, immediately
astern, coming sideways with a hissing indrawn breath and a
curl of white on its forehead. So I had to nurse the boat over
that and over two more big ones and when I looked again the
bird had gone.

To beware of being moon-fey a second time I sat on the other
side and steered by the compass and by Capella that shone bright
in the sky. We were far from any boat track and it was easy to
imagine anything at night and alone on the sea. Our boat was so
tiny, such a duckling of a craft, shaped childishly like the moon
above me or like a pre-historic drawing of the boat in which the
sun-myth hero makes his sea journey, that it became impossible
not to think anthropomorphically. I had convinced myself that
our journey to the west, like the sun's, was symbolical, that the
moon had evil desires on me and that if I stared at her boat much

longer mooncraft would prevail and I would be infecundated according to some magical ritual which unconsciously I was following and into whose circle I had stepped when we sailed into that name of magic, the Arafura Sea. The Arafura Sea ringed about with savage lands, one of the most primitive of which we had just left.

So I practised an exorcism of my own, repeating to myself such fragments of poetry about the moon as swam into my head. Presently I became tired; my back ached; my head, bedazzled by moon and the light of the binnacle lamp on the jigging compass card, ached too. I looked at the time. I had forty minutes to go. How wearily they dragged. One could always tell when the steersman was getting tired. He would ask the time or keep bending to look at the watch that hung in the galley.

When at last it was time to wake Sven I was glad. He came up sleepy and I noticed that he had on his bathing suit. Ready for the worst in case he had to swim? No. Had the Chuchu at Merauke stolen his pyjamas? No. It was merely that in rough weather he rarely undressed because he was called up so frequently and the woollen bathing suit was the only warm clothing he had left that was dry.

We had our cycle of awakenings. Henery woke Ruth and was wakened by Joan. He slept heavily and an ordinary call would not rouse him, the cycle was arranged so that Joan should suffer if he didn't come up. She managed to wake him quietly. In her turn she was wakened by Sven, whom I woke, while Ruth woke me. The cook for the next day always dropped out the night watch before his cookday and the awakening process stepped on one. The arrangements worked.

On the fourth morning out I still had a store throat. I fed myself on hot milk and soup made from a set of powders with different labels but all exactly the same, looking, tasting, and smelling like liquorice powder. Their main virtue was that they were hot and slimy. The sea was a deep bottle-green. Joan was the only one still sea-sick. On our dead reckoning we were due to sight the south-eastern extremity of the Aru group round which we had to shape our course, but there was no sign of land and an overcast sky still prevented Sven from taking a sight.

Next morning, August 25th, land appeared. We had rounded the point of the Arus and completed the run of five hundred miles in four days. We had come to Dobo. We had lost nothing except our starboard name-plate; it had come off in the battering.

SCENE TWO:
A STORM AT SEA

NICHOLAS MONSARRAT

Nicholas Monsarrat was born in Liverpool in 1910, educated at Cambridge, then moved to London, where he wrote three novels before entering the Royal Navy Volunteer Reserve during the Second World War. He served on the corvettes and frigates that escorted convoys of supply ships between Halifax and England, and later wrote *Three Corvettes,* a non-fiction account of his experiences. After the war he published *The Cruel Sea* (1951), a work of fiction about the convoy service and a vivid portrayal of life aboard a small ship in the North Atlantic. He subsequently held diplomatic posts in South Africa and Ottawa. Monsarrat spent his final years in Malta; when he died in 1979, he was given an honorary burial at sea by the Royal Navy.

. . .

SCENE TWO: A STORM at Sea. Enter a Ship, hard-driven, labouring... But even that simple directive could not be obeyed, because no ship could enter, no ship could make a foot of headway on to any stage like this. The storm-scene itself would have to move to meet the ship—and that, thought Ericson, when the fifth dawn in succession found his ship still fighting a fantastic battle to force her way even as far south as Iceland, that reversal of nature was not impossible; for here must be the worst weather of the war, the worst weather in the world.

It was more than a full gale at sea, it was nearer to a great roaring battlefield with ships blowing across it like scraps of newspaper. The convoy no longer had the shape of a convoy, and indeed a ship was scarcely a ship, trapped and hounded in this howling wilderness. The tumult of that southerly gale, increasing in fury from day to day, had a staggering malice from which there was no escape: it was as if each ship were some desperate fugitive, sentenced to be lynched by a mob whose movements had progressed from clumsy ill-humour to sightless rage.

Huge waves, a mile from crest to crest, roared down upon the pigmies that were to be their prey; sometimes the entire surface of the water would be blown bodily away, and any ship that stood in the path of the onslaught shook and staggered as tons of green sea smote her upper deck and raced in a torrent down her whole length. Boats were smashed, funnels were buckled, bridges and deck-houses were crushed out of shape: men disappeared overboard without a trace and without a cry, sponged out of life like figures wiped from a blackboard at a single impervious stroke. Even when the green seas withheld their blows for a moment, the wind, screaming and clawing at the rigging, struck fear into every heart; for if deck-gear and canvas screens could vanish, perhaps even men could be whipped away by its furious strength . . . For the crew of *Saltash*, there was no convoy, and no other ships save their own; and she, and they, were caught in a mesh of fearful days and nights, which might defeat them by their sheer brutal force. Normally a good sea boat, *Saltash* had ridden out many storms and had often had strength to spare for other ships that might be in difficulties; now, entirely on her own, she laboured to stay afloat, wearily performing, for hour after hour and day after day, the ugly antics of a ship which refused, under the most desperate compulsion, to stand on her head.

Throughout it all, the ship's relay-loudspeaker system, monotonously fed by a satirical hand, boomed out a tune called *Someone's Rocking My Dream-boat.*

Each of them in the wardroom had problems of a special sort to cope with, over and above the ones they shared with the rest of the crew—the problem of eating without having food flung in their faces, of sleeping without being thrown out of their bunks, of getting warm and dry again after the misery of a four-hour watch: above all, the problem of staying unhurt.

Scott-Brown, the doctor, was kept busy with this human wreckage of the storm, treating from hour to hour the cuts, the cracked ribs, the seasickness that could exhaust a man beyond the wish to live. His worst casualty, the one which would have needed all his skill and patience even if he had been able to deal with it in a quiet, fully-equipped operating-theatre ashore, was a man who, thrown bodily from one side of the mess-deck to the other, had landed on his knee-cap and smashed it into a dozen bloody fragments.

Johnson, the engineer officer, had a problem calling for end-less watchfulness—the drunken movements of the ship, which brought her stern high out of the water with every second wave, and could set the screws racing and tearing the shaft to bits unless the throttle were clamped down straight away.

Raikes, in charge of navigation, was confronted by a truly hopeless job. For days on end there had been no sun to shoot, no stars to be seen, no set speed to give him even a rough D.R. position: where *Saltash* had got to, after five days and nights of chaos, was a matter of pure guess-work which any second-class stoker, pin in hand, could have done just as well as he. Ill-balanced on the Arctic Circle, sixty-something North by nothing West—that was the nearest he could get to it: *Saltash* lay somewhere inside those ragged limits, drifting slowly backwards within the wild triangle of Iceland, Jan Meyen Island, and Norway.

The ship's organization was, as usual, Lockhart's respon-sibility; and the ship's organization had become a wicked sort of joke. Between decks, *Saltash* was in chaos—the wardroom uninhabitable, the mess-decks a shambles: there could be no hot food, no way of drying clothes, no comfort for anyone under the ceaseless battering of the storm. Deck-gear worked loose, boats jumped their chocks and battered themselves to bits, water fell in solid tons on every part of the ship: after facing with hope a thousand dawns, Lockhart now dreaded what might meet his eye at the end of his watch, when daylight pierced the wild and lowering sky and showed him the ship again. An upper deck swept clean, a whole batch of thirty seamen vanished overboard—these were the outlines of a waking nightmare which might, with a single turn of fortune, come hideously true.

As *Saltash* laboured, as *Saltash* faltered and groaned, as *Saltash* found each tortured dawn no better than the last, he, along with the rest, could only endure, and curse the cruel sea.

No one cursed it with more cause and with less public demonstration than Ericson, who, self-locked into one corner of the bridge, was fulfilling once more his traditional rôle of holding the whole thing together. After five days and nights of storm, he was so exhausted that the feeling of exhaustion had virtually disappeared: anchored to the deck by lead-like legs and soaked sea-boots, clamped to the bridge by weary half-frozen arms, he seemed to have become a part of the ship herself—a fixed pair of eyes, a watchful brain welded into the fabric of *Saltash*. All the way north to Murmansk he had had to perform the mental acrobatics necessary to the control of twenty escorts and the repelling of three or four different kinds of attack: now the physical harassing of this monstrous gale was battering at his body in turn, sapping at a life-time's endurance which had never had so testing a call made upon it, had never had to cope with an ordeal on this scale.

Assaulted by noise, bruised and punished by frenzied movement, thrown about endlessly, he had to watch and feel the same things happening to his ship.

The scene from the bridge of *Saltash* never lost an outline of senseless violence. By day it showed a square mile of tormented water, with huge waves flooding in like mountains sliding down to the surface of the earth: with a haze of spray and spume scudding across it continually: with gulfs opening before the ship as if the whole ocean was avid to swallow her. Outlined against a livid sky, the mast plunged and rocked through a wild arc of space, flinging the aerials and the signal halyards about as if to whip the sea for its wickedness. Night added the terrible unknown; night was pitch-black, unpierceable to the eye, inhabited by fearful noises and sudden treacherous surprises: by waves that crashed down from nowhere, by stinging spray that tore into a man's face and eyes before he could duck for shelter. Isolated in the blackness, *Saltash* suffered every assault: she pitched, she rolled, she laboured: she met the shock of a breaking wave with a jar that shook her from end to end, she dived shuddering into a deep trough, shipping tons of water with a noise like a collapsing house, and then rose with infinite slowness, infinite pain, to shoulder the mass of water aside, and shake herself free, and prepare herself for the next blow.

Ericson watched and suffered with her, and felt it all in his own body: felt especially the agony of that slow rise under the crushing weight of the sea, felt often the enormous doubt as to whether she would rise at all. Ships had foundered without trace in this sort of weather: ships could give up, and lie down under punishment, just as could human beings: here, in this high corner of the world where the weather had started to scream insanely and the sea to boil, here could be murder: here, where some of *Compass Rose*'s corpses might still be wandering, here he might join them, with yet another ship's company in his train.

He stayed where he was on the bridge, and waited for it to happen, or not to happen. He was a pair of red eyes, inflamed by wind and salt water: he was a brain, tired, fluttering, but forced into a channel of watchfulness: he was sometimes a voice, shouting to the helmsman below to prepare for another threatening blow from the sea. He was a core of fear and of control, clipped small and tight into a body he had first ill-treated, and then begun, perforce, to disregard.

THE ENDURING SEA

———

RACHEL CARSON

Born on a farm near Springdale, Pennsylvania, in 1907, Rachel Carson graduated with a degree in zoology from Johns Hopkins University and in 1936 became the first full-time woman biologist with the U.S. Bureau of Fisheries. By 1949 she was the chief editor of all U.S. Fish and Wildlife Service publications, and in 1952 left the Service to concentrate on her own writing. She had already published *Under the Sea Wind* (1941) and *The Sea Around Us* (1952), and went on to write *The Edge of the Sea* (1955), from which this haunting description of "that great mother of life, the sea," is taken. Her groundbreaking work, *Silent Spring* (1962), is credited with launching the global environmental movement. She died in Silver Spring, Maryland, in 1964.

. . .

NOW I HEAR the sea sounds about me; the night high tide is rising, swirling with a confused rush of waters against the rocks below my study window. Fog has come into the bay from the open sea, and it lies over water and over the land's edge, seeping back into the spruces and stealing softly among the juniper and the bayberry. The restive waters, the cold wet breath of the fog, are of a world in which man is an uneasy trespasser; he punctuates the night with the complaining groan and grunt of a foghorn, sensing the power and menace of the sea.

Hearing the rising tide, I think how it is pressing also against other shores I know—rising on a southern beach where there is no fog, but a moon edging all the waves with silver and touching the wet sands with lambent sheen, and on a still more distant shore sending its streaming currents against the moonlit pinnacles and the dark caves of the coral rock.

Then in my thoughts these shores, so different in their nature and in the inhabitants they support, are made one by the unifying touch of the sea. For the differences I sense in this particular instant of time that is mine are but the differences of a moment, determined by our place in the stream of time and in the long rhythms of the sea. Once this rocky coast beneath me was a plain of sand; then the sea rose and found a new shore line. And again in some shadowy future the surf will have ground these rocks to sand and they will have returned the coast to its earliest state. And so in my mind's eye these coastal forms merge and blend in a shifting, kaleidoscopic pattern in which there is no finality, no ultimate and fixed reality—earth becoming fluid as the sea itself.

On all these shores there are echoes of past and future; of the flow of time, obliterating yet containing all that has gone before; all the sea's eternal rhythms—the tides, the beat of surf, the pressing rivers of the currents—shaping, changing, dominating; of the stream of life, flowing as inexorably as any ocean current, from past to unknown future. For as the shore configuration changes in the flow of time, the pattern of life changes, never static, never quite the same from year to year. Whenever the sea builds a new coast, the waves of living creatures surge against it, seeking a foothold, establishing their colonies. And so we come to perceive life as a force as tangible as any of the physical realities of the sea, a force strong and purposeful, as incapable of being crushed or diverted from its ends as the rising tide.

Contemplating the teeming life of the shore, we have an uneasy sense of the communication of some universal truth that lies just beyond our grasp. What is the message signalled in the night sea? What truth is expressed by the legions of the barnacles, whitening the rocks with their habitations, each small creature within finding the necessities of its existence in the sweep of the surf? And what is the meaning of so tiny a being as the transparent wisp of protoplasm that is a sea lace, existing for some reason inscrutable to us—a reason that demands its presence by the trillion amid the rocks and weeds of the shore? The meaning haunts and ever eludes us, and in its very pursuit we approach the ultimate mystery of Life itself.

THE WRECKER
IN ALL OF US

JOHN FOWLES

John Fowles (1926–2005), best known as the author of such novels as *The Collector* (1963), *The Magus* (1965), and *The French Lieutenant's Woman* (1969), was also a prolific writer of creative nonfiction. He wrote the text for two elegant photographic essays—*Islands* (1978, with photographs by Fay Godwin) and *The Tree* (1979, photographs by Frank Horvat)—and the introduction to *Shipwreck* (1974), a book of shipwreck photographs taken since the 1860s by three generations of the Gibson family on the Isles of Scilly. In this excerpt from that essay, Fowles ruminates on the fascination that shipwrecks—indeed all natural disasters, but especially those at sea— excite in our imaginations. Fowles lived in Lyme Regis, a picturesque town on the Devonshire coast of England, until his death on November 5, 2005.

. . .

THERE IS, FROM dry land, great poetry and drama about the shipwreck; but no sailor would let me suggest that the amusement of an audience is the heart of the matter. That heart lies, as it always has lain and always will lie, in the terror and despair, in the drowned, in the appalling suffering of the survived, the bravery of the rescuers. We should never forget that; and yet . . . I should like to go now into the calmer, though deeper and darker, waters of why the spectacle of the shipwreck is so pleasing—why, in short, there is a kind of Cornish wrecker in every single one of us.

OUR PRIVATE attitude towards communal disaster, the joint death of other people, could be regarded as unalloyedly humanitarian only by a supreme optimist; yet I should not like to call it, short of the pathological extreme, unhealthy. There is the Christian view: we feel pity for the victims. There is the Aristotelian: we feel purged, and go away better people. And so on, until we come down to the cynical: it is all a matter of schadenfreude, and at least the population problem is relieved a little. But I'm not sure that the most important reaction is not the instinctive: thank God this did not happen to me. In other words, we derive from the spectacle of calamity a sense of personal survival—as also, however tenuously, intimations of the metaphysical sea of hazard on which we all sail.

Perhaps one should not distinguish among train and air crashes, motorway pileups, and all the other downstrokes that the traveler is prone to; yet there is something rather special about the shipwreck, and I think not simply because it usually has a longer agony and a longer aftermath than death on land and in the air. The sea seems less greedy, for a start. Humanity's ability to endure in it against all the odds is a strange and incalculable thing: so many drowned men have crawled up a beach or been picked up in small boats weeks after they were consigned by all probability to Davy Jones's bottomless locker. But more important—at least for us spectators—than this intermittent show of mercy is surely the emotional symbolism.

This springs from two things: the nature of the sea and the nature of the ship. No other element has such accreted layers of significance for us, such complex archetypal meaning. The sea's moods and uses sex it. It is the great creatrix, feeder, womb and vagina, place of pleasure; the gentlest thing on earth, the most maternal; the most seductive whore, and handsomely the most faithless. It has the attributes of all women, and all men too. It can be subtle and noble, brave and energetic; and far crueler than the meanest, most sadistic human king who ever ruled. ("I believe in the Bible," an old sailor once told Lord Fisher, "because it don't mention no sea in Paradise.") I happen to live over the sea myself; I watch it every day, I hear it every night. I do not like it angry, but I've noticed that most urban and inland people adore it so. Storms and gales seem to awaken something joyous and excited in them: the thunder on the shingle, the spray and spume, the rut and rage.

No doubt this is partly a product of a life where the elements have largely receded out of daily notice; but I think it goes deeper, into a kind of Freudian double identification, in which the wrath of the sea is interpreted both as superego and as id. It is on the one hand a thing without restraint, a giant bull in a salt ring; on the other it is the great punisher of presumption, the patriarch who cuts that green stripling, man, down to size. It is strangely—or perhaps not so strangely, in these days of the universal oil slick—as if we had committed a crime against the sea by ever leaving it in the first place; and as if we liked to be told (through convenient scapegoats, of course) that we merit retribution for our ambitious folly. In its rages, we admire the total lack of reason and justice, the blindness to all but the laws of its own nature; and quite naturally, since similar feelings and desires lurk deep inside our own minds. A wrecking sea is part of what we all dream ourselves to be every night; and the ship becomes our own puny calculations, our repressions, our compromises, our kow-towings to convention, duty, and a dozen other idols of the top-hamper we call civilization. A psychiatrist tells me that a morbid obsession with disaster is a common defense against depression; its enjoyment brings a vicarious sense of manic triumph over normal reality. So the shipwreck is not only what we are thankful will never happen to us; it is also what we secretly want to happen, and finally to ourselves.

The other great nexus of metaphors and feelings is the ship itself. No human invention, with all its associated crafts in building and handling, has an older history—or has received more love. That is why we have sexed it without ambiguity, at least in the West; which in this context casts the sea, the domain of Neptune, as raper, berserker, Bluebeard. Even our judgment of a ship's beauty has tended to be that of the male upon the female—that is, we put a greater value on outward line than on soul or utility, and nowhere more than with the last of the sailing ships, that splendid and sharply individualized zenith of five thousand years' worth of hard-earned knowledge and aesthetic instinct. The vocabulary of the aeroplane seduced us for a while; but I think it is interesting that we have come back to star- and space-*ships*. *Jet* will do for a transport shorthand; yet when man really reaches, across the vast seas of space, he still reaches in ships. Other words may function as well; no other has the poetries.

All this leads me to believe that there is, with the kind of shipwreck I have been talking about here, a nobler constituent in our fascination: a genuine sadness. They are lost craft in both senses of the noun; they are failed hopes, ventures, destinies, but also shattered monuments to countless generations of anonymous shipwrights and sailmakers, as tragic in their way as the vanished masterpieces of great sculptors.

Just as there are found objects, so there are agonized ones. The mist comes down on the drowned *Mildred*, her masts and ultimate sails rise from the appeased water like an epitaph, a cross of remembrance, a lovely assemblage of rope construct and canvas cutout, pre-echoing Matisse and Naum Gabo . . . We have our monuments to the Unknown Soldier; will anyone ever give us a more beautiful celebration of the Lost Ship?

THE SEA IS HISTORY

DEREK WALCOTT

Caribbean poet and playwright Derek Walcott was born in 1930 in Castries, St. Lucia. He attended the University of the West Indies in Jamaica and moved to Trinidad in 1953. Today he divides his time between Trinidad and Boston, and teaches poetry and playwriting at Boston University. He has written more than thirty plays, and in 1959 he founded the Trinidad Theatre Workshop. His long poem *Omeros,* a retelling of the *Iliad* and the *Odyssey* in a Caribbean setting, appeared in 1990; in 1992 he was awarded the Nobel Prize for Literature. "The Sea Is History," included in his *Collected Poems 1948–1984* (1986), makes the point that, to descendants of Caribbean slaves, the sea is both the element that cut them off from their history and the only history they have.

. . .

Where are your monuments, your battles, martyrs?
Where is your tribal memory? Sirs,
in that grey vault. The sea. The sea
has locked them up. The sea is History.

First, there was the heaving oil,
heavy as chaos;
then, like a light at the end of a tunnel,

the lantern of a caravel,
and that was Genesis.
Then there were the packed cries,
the shit, the moaning:

Exodus.
Bone soldered by coral to bone,
mosaics
mantled by the benediction of the shark's shadow,

that was the Ark of the Covenant.
Then came from the plucked wires
of sunlight on the sea floor

the plangent harps of the Babylonian bondage,
as the white cowries clustered like manacles
on the drowned women,

and those were the ivory bracelets
of the Song of Solomon,
but the ocean kept turning blank pages

looking for History.
Then came the men with eyes heavy as anchors
who sank without tombs,

brigands who barbecued cattle,
leaving their charred ribs like palm leaves on the shore,
then the foaming, rabid maw

of the tidal wave swallowing Port Royal,
and that was Jonah,
but where is your Renaissance?

Sir, it is locked in them sea-sands
out there past the reef's moiling shelf
where the men-o'-war floated down;

strop on these goggles, I'll guide you there myself.
It's all subtle and submarine,
through colonnades of coral,

past the gothic windows of sea-fans
to where the crusty grouper, onyx-eyed,
blinks, weighted by its jewels, like a bald queen;

and these groined caves with barnacles
pitted like stone
are our cathedrals,

and the furnace before the hurricanes:
Gomorrah. Bones ground by windmills
into marl and cornmeal,

and that was Lamentations—
that was just Lamentations,
it was not History;

then came, like the scum on the river's drying lip,
the brown reeds of villages
mantling and congealing into towns,

and at evening, the midge's choirs,
and above them, the spire
lancing the side of God

as His son set, and that was the New Testament.

Then came the white sisters clapping
to the waves' progress,
and that was Emancipation—

jubilation, O jubilation—
vanishing swiftly
as the sea's lace dries in the sun,

but that was not History,
that was only faith,
and then each rock broke into its own nation;

then came the synod of flies,
then came the secretarial heron,
then came the bullfrog bellowing for a vote,

fireflies with bright ideas
and bats like jetting ambassadors
and the mantis, like khaki police,

and the furred caterpillars of judges
examining each case closely,
and then in the dark ears of ferns

and in the salt chuckle of rocks
with their sea pools, there was the sound
like a rumour without any echo

of History, really beginning.

THE BOAT JOURNEY

ANDREA BARRETT

Andrea Barrett was born in 1954, grew up with the sea in Cape Cod, and studied biology at Union College in Schenectady, New York, with the intention of becoming "a Darwin in skirts." Indeed, science informs her novels and short stories: *Lucid Stars* (1988); *Secret Harmonies* (1989), *The Middle Kingdom* (1991), and *The Forms of Water* (1993) all deal with themes arising from scientific knowledge. Her 1996 short-story collection *Ship Fever* was highly acclaimed, as was her novel of hardship and heroism in the high Arctic, *The Voyage of the Narwhal* (1998), from which this passage, describing a grueling forced march over breaking ice, is taken. One of her most recent novels, *Servants of the Map* (2002), was a finalist for the Pulitzer Prize. Barrett lives in North Adams, Massachusetts.

. . .

LATER, DIFFERENT SCENES from the boat journey would float back to each of them. So much work, so much pain; so little rest or food or hope. What happened when? What happened in fact, and what was only imagined, or misremembered? Erasmus made no diary entries, nor did Ned or the other men. Of the days when they were out on the ice, heaving against the harnesses and rowing through lanes of ice-choked water, or sleeping packed like a litter of piglets inside the canvas-covered boat, nothing remained but a blur of impressions.

From their cove down the ice belt to Cape Sabine, then across the broken, heaving Sound to a point slightly north of Cape Hatherton: pack ice, water, old ice, hummocks, thin ice, pressure ridges. Always pulling, except for the wearying, exasperating times when their way was blocked by an open channel and they must unload everything, remove the boat from the sledge, ferry across, reload, and begin the whole process again. Their shoulders and hands were rubbed raw by the ropes, and Ivan would remember the acid burn of vomit on his lips; they all threw up, they were pulling too much weight. Near the leads the ice was covered with slush and often they sank above their knees. Sean would remember how his ankles ballooned, forcing him to slit his boots and finally cut them off entirely, so that he made the rest of the journey with his feet wrapped in caribou hides. Robert would remember his persistent, burning diarrhea, and the humiliation of soiling his pants when he strained against the weight of the sledge.

Erasmus would pause one day after skidding helplessly on the ice, and then he'd think of the bit of boot sole sealed in his box and wonder why they hadn't all thought to stud their boots similarly. In what seemed to him now like another life, his boots had shot him off the face of a cliff—and still he hadn't learned. But it was too late now, they had no screws; they fell and stumbled and were relieved only once, when the ice field was smooth and the wind blew from the northwest. That day they set the sails and glided for eight miles: a great blessing, never repeated, which Barton would dream about for years.

From a high point of land on the Greenland side of Smith Sound, Captain Tyler and Mr. Tagliabeau saw more ice south of them, but also, in the distance, an open channel between the land-fast ice and the pack ice slicing southward. Isaac, blinded by the snow, would not remember this sight, but the others would; and Thomas would remember his frantic rush, at night when he was already exhausted, to caulk the boat's seams and repair the holes. And how anxious he'd felt when Erasmus told him they all depended on his ability to keep the boat together with no proper supplies.

At the Littleton Islands the ice field thinned, abraded from beneath by the currents from a nearby river. Barton would remember inching forward the last few miles, sounding the ice with a boat hook at every step and eying the eddies gurgling just below his feet. And then breaking through, despite his precautions: one side of the sledge crashing under, the sickening lurch and the scramble to firmer ice. Ivan remembered that moment— always, always—because he'd been tied in closest to the sledge and, as his companions heaved, had lost his footing and been pulled into the water, to bob briefly under the edge of the ice. By the time Erasmus pulled him out by the hair, he'd broken two fingers and seen blood pour from a gash in Erasmus's forehead. In the ice-choked water Erasmus floundered, scrambling for the provision bags slithering out of the boat as the sea slithered over the sides. The copper pot containing the Franklin relics slipped out too, but the air beneath the walrus skin kept it floating low in the water and at first Erasmus thought he might retrieve it. Under the broken floe it sailed, the floe that had nearly claimed Ivan; and although Erasmus pressed his shoulder against the edge and swept with his arm and then a paddle, finally lowering his head beneath the ice, the pot disappeared. That night a hard wind blew from the northeast, nearly freezing the wet men to death.

Erasmus would remember this because it was here that he lost the evidence of their search for Franklin's remains, and also because, although he could never be sure, he suspected that here began the process of freezing and constriction and infection that would later cause him to lose his toes. He should have been resting, with his boots removed and his feet wrapped in dry furs. But instead, that night he and Captain Tyler, with whom he'd been arguing since they left the brig, stood screaming at each other in front of the men and nearly came to blows. Each blamed the other for the accident and the loss of the relics—as each had blamed the other for every wrong turn taken, bad camping site chosen, failure hunting—and Captain Tyler had slashed the air with a boathook and said, "I despise you." A moment that Mr. Tagliabeau, never more than a few feet from his captain but less and less certain that his loyalty was justified, would also always remember. He'd longed to turn his back and say, "I despise you both," but had said nothing; on this journey he learned that he was both a coward and a complainer.

Not long after that accident, though, they stood on a high mound and saw a lane of open water spreading before them. With much effort they made their way to a rocky beach, and then unloaded the boat for the last time and sank it for a day to swell the seams. Not long enough, Thomas would remember thinking. The surf was beating against the cliffs; was it his fault the boat still leaked when it was finally, properly launched? They were ten men in a whale boat made for six, with too much baggage. Trembling inches above the water they rowed, and felt like they were swimming. Under reefed sails, in a fresh breeze, they rounded Cape Alexander.

Ned would remember the mock sun that appeared in the sky that evening; a perfect parhelion—Dr. Boerhaave had taught him that word—with a point of light on either side. But neither Ned nor anyone else would be haunted by the sight of Dr. Boerhaave's head, which in the months since his drowning had been severed from his body by a passing grampus and then swept south in the currents, coming to rest face up on the rubble below a cliff. Among the rounded rocks his head was invisible to his friends, and the singing noise made by the wind passing over his jaw bones was lost in the roar of the waves.

Sutherland Island, where they'd hoped to land, was barricaded by ice. They bobbed all night in irregular winds and a violent freezing rain, and Ned would remember this place for the weather and the onset of his fever, which caused this journey to be jumbled forever after in his mind with his two earlier crossings of Smith Sound. Eastward with Joe and Dr. Boerhaave and Zeke he'd gone; westward with only Zeke. He remembered that. Pushing like an animal against the harness, pulling the sledge sunk into the soft surface—those journeys, or this journey?

Once the worst of the fever hit and he lay helpless among his companions, he repeated to himself the stories Joe had told him as they pulled another sledge, in another month. The stories that, once they reached Anoatok, Joe had translated for him around the fire. They'd lain on a platform inside the hut, mashed in a crowd of Esquimaux and sharing walrus steaks. Meat was piled along the ice belt and walrus skulls glared eyeless from the snowbanks. A mighty spirit called *Tonarsuk,* Joe had said, spearing a morsel from the soup pot. In whom these Esquimaux believe. And many minor supernatural beings, chief among them the goblins known as *innersuit,* who live among the fjords and have no noses. The *innersuit* hide behind the rocks, waiting to capture a passing man so they may cut off his nose and force him to join their tribe. Should the victim escape their clutches, his nose may be returned to him by the intercession of a skillful wizard, or *angekok*. The nose may come back, Joe had said; he'd been translating Ootuniah's words for Ned and Dr. Boerhaave, as they steamed companionably in the hut. The nose may come flying through the sky, and settle down in its former place; but the man once captured by the *innersuit* will always be known by the scar across his face.

Ned's fever, or frostbite, or something putrid he ate, had caused his own nose to erupt in pustules that leaked yellow fluid and then crusted over and cracked and bled. He would remember dreading his whole nose might disappear. And then thinking it *should* disappear—along with his face, his entire body: Who was to blame for all this, if not him? He had lied to Erasmus; he'd made those fur suits and shifted supplies like a thief; he'd planned this trip and organized the men. On Boothia, he'd pointed out the copper kettles that had set everything else in motion; on his earlier crossing of the Sound, he'd failed to save Dr. Boerhaave. As they passed fjords and glaciers he heard singing—not Dr. Boerhaave, but someone else—and begged the man against whose knee he was pressed to guard him from the goblins. The *innersuit* cause much trouble, Ootuniah had said. They plague many a journey. Weeping with guilt and fear, his hands cupped over his nose, Ned remembered his grandmother's tales back in Ireland. Malicious spirits who made porridge burn, toast fall buttered side down, cows lose their calves. Perhaps it was the *innersuit* who'd haunted this journey and brought the fickle, difficult weather.

Perhaps, he told Erasmus one night—perhaps it was the *innersuit* who were to blame for their bad luck. They pushed through half-solid water, around icebergs and currents of drift ice. One night they anchored in a crack as a gale struck from the northwest, watching helplessly as a floe on the far side of the channel broke off, spun on an iceberg like a pivot, and closed upon their resting place. When it hit the corner of their small dock the floe shattered, their haven shattered, everything around them rose and crushed and tumbled. The boat was tossed like a walnut shell into a boiling slurry of crushed ice and water, and Robert would remember his more sharply than the other accidents, because it was here that he dislocated his shoulder. Captain Tyler held him down while Erasmus torqued his arm back into place, and Robert would remember being amazed, even through the blinding pain, that the pair had worked in concert.

On Hakluyt Island they found birds, but failed to shoot any. A seal they shot near an iceberg sank before they could retrieve it. They ran out of food, for a week eating only a few ounces of bread dust and pemmican each day with all of them feverish, all of them weak, and Ned muttered that perhaps the *innersuit* had stolen Joe from them, and tipped Dr. Boerhaave into the water. Erasmus would remember this comment and how sharply it pained him. Despite his worry for Ned, and for the others who didn't understand how weak they'd grown but were each day less capable, still the mention of Dr. Boerhaave could make his mind freeze up. He never thought about Zeke, the thought was impossible; he hardly thought about what was happening to his feet, although they were oozing and stinking and numb; he focused on getting them all through each day, pushing forward and cooking and eating and resting and pushing again, putting the miles behind them. But when Ned muttered about goblins and Dr. Boerhaave, Erasmus had to fight to keep his concentration.

Northumberland Island, Whale Sound, Cape Parry. The sea was covered with drifting pack ice, which poured from Whale Sound in a constant stream. At night thin ice formed in the open patches, and Erasmus would remember the panic this caused him. If they were caught here they would never survive; and Ned would be the first to go. Ned was delirious, and when Robert and Ivan shot a heap of dovekies, Ned sat upright, his nose a bloody, eroded mass, and babbled. Something about a great hunt: he and Joe and Dr. Boerhaave joining the Esquimaux on the cliffs where the dovekies were breeding. Sweeping the birds from the air with nets at the end of long narwhal tusks; thousands caught as easily as one might pick peas and the bodies boiling in huge soapstone pots, the children sucking on bird skins and tearing raw birds limb from limb, their faces buried in feathers and blood smeared over their cheeks. But Ned wouldn't eat these other birds, he couldn't bear to bring food near his nose. He said names, only some of which Erasmus knew—Awahtok, Metek, Ootuniah; Myouk, Egurk, Nualik, Nessark—and later, when those names and the people behind them would return to haunt Erasmus, he'd remember envying Ned all he'd seen on that trip, and wishing yet again that he'd been present: Dr. Boerhaave might still be alive.

Erasmus both heard and didn't hear Ned as he forced the boat farther south. Captain Tyler and Mr. Tagliabeau contradicted his every order, more and more confident as they passed Hoppner Point and Granville Bay and it began to seem that, if they could just beat the final freezing-in, they might actually reach the whaling grounds. They were racing, racing, the temperature dropping each day and the new ice forming, the pack consolidating, the narrow channel closing: yet despite the urgency Captain Tyler argued over every tack and turn. These were his waters, Erasmus would remember him saying; they were in his country now and Erasmus must cede command to him. Here he knew what was best for the expedition.

Erasmus had unlaced his boots that morning, unable to resist confirming by eye what he could already feel; eight of his toes were black and dead. In Dr. Boerhaave's medicine chest were amputating knives, still sharp and gleaming, but it was impossible that he should use them on himself. It was also now impossible that he should walk any distance if the ice closed around them, but no one knew that yet. Or maybe Captain Tyler did know; he seemed to sense Erasmus's growing weakness.

"You refused to lead the men earlier," Erasmus would remember saying to the captain. "When the men most needed you, you'd do nothing. Now that there's a chance we might reach safety you want command, you want the credit." The rifles and powder and shot were scattered throughout the boat, but he had all the percussion caps and felt secure. "I'll shoot you if you disobey me," he said.

All the men would remember that: how nearly they'd come to having to choose sides, how only a waving gun had saved them. For the last few days, creeping around Cape Dudley Digges and then through a narrow lead at the base of the ice foot, no one spoke except to give or respond to orders. Every night the temperature dropped below freezing, although it was still warm at noon. Sometimes it snowed. They rowed through a dense sludge that dripped from the oars like porridge, and when at last they doubled Cape York they dreaded the emptiness. October 3, Melville Bay. Upernavik, on the far side of the breaking-up yard, was still so many miles away.

SKY LIKE A GRUBBY
WASHCLOTH

JONATHAN RABAN

Born in Norfolk, England, in 1942, Jonathan Raban attended the University of Hull and taught English literature in Wales and at the University of East Anglia. In 1969, he moved to London to become a freelance writer. *Soft City*, his affectionate celebration of urban life, appeared in 1974, followed by such modern travel classics as *Old Glory: An American Voyage* (1981), *Bad Land: An American Romance* (1996), and the book from which this excerpt, about the effect of tides, is taken, *Passage to Juneau: A Sea and Its Meanings* (1999). The latter follows Raban's solo voyage from his current home in Seattle up the West Coast's inland passage to Alaska. Raban is also the editor of *The Oxford Book of the Sea* (1992).

. . .

0645. BAR. 998, r. Sky like a grubby washcloth, draped low over the trees. Dead calm. Forecast wind: NW10–15.

IN THE chill of what passed in Blind Channel for dawn, the blood had bypassed the tips of three of my fingers, which made writing difficult, and gave my extremities the appearance of belonging to someone else's corpse. Gripping a mug of hot coffee to coax the pink back into my fingertips, I pulled away from the dock and began a stopwatch race against the tide. Greene Point Rapids, just around the corner, turned at nearly the same moment as Whirlpool Rapids, twelve miles further on. By taking the first set on the flood, an hour and ten minutes before slack, I hoped to shoot the second on ebb, within an hour of the turn.

Greene Point Rapids was a long, straight, gleaming hill of water, where the tide surged through the gap between West Thurlow and the Cordero Islands. Seabirds had stained the cluster of spiky rocks to starboard a uniform white, and the usual foul-tempered mob was rioting over the bonbons cast up by the turbulent deep. The boat labored against the gradient, barely gaining on the beacon where two sated cormorants were perched, digesting their breakfast fish. Seven knots through the water; two, at best, over the ground. The diesel snarled underfoot at maximum revs. Blue smoke swirled astern and came drifting back into the cockpit. The cormorants, hanging their wings out to dry, inched past the bow to the shrouds, then drew level with the doghouse: a pair of miniature black pterodactyls with prehistoric eyes.

I was surprised by the force of the tide as it drove deep inland, but was able to keep the boat more or less on course, with only an occasional sideways slew as it skidded on a boil. The gulls' clamor and thrashing wings made it hard to read the water surface and locate the back-eddies to the side of the main stream, but the beacon slid gradually astern and the current soon weakened to a manageable three and a half knots.

In the stories I'd been reading, the tide was the most nearly friendly to humans of all the powers of nature. Though it had not always been so: once upon a time, control of the tides had been in the hands of famously vindictive beings: South Wind (Puget Sound Salish); West Wind (Nootka); Thunder-Eagle (Coos and Tillamook); Wolf (Kwakiutl); or the Mistress of the Tides, the ancient hag who held the "tide-line" in her hands and could let it out or draw it up at will (Tsimshian and Tlingit). In those days, the sea sometimes rose so high as to drown the mountains, or withdrew so far as to leave the whole country parched and dying. Then someone—usually Raven, though sometimes Halibut, Skate, or Mink—tricked or blackmailed the tyrant power into moderating the tide and putting it on a regular daily basis with strict limits to the extent of high water, so that Indians could safely gather shellfish from the beaches during an ebb tide, without fear that their villages might be inundated by the coming flood.

It was obvious why people thought the tides of the past much fiercer than those of the present: a bull tide, when the sun and moon lined up on one axis, came roaring through these narrow channels as if nothing short of miraculous intervention could ever stanch it. Most coastal tribes had stories of a great flood long ago, when the sea swamped the world and left canoes stranded on snowpeaks. The missionaries found Noah was a surefire hit on the reservations; one had only to see a spring tide in action here to start thinking of arks and Ararats.

In this habitually overcast country, where a week might go by without a glimmer of sun or stars, the best available way of telling the time was by tide. In Halkomelem, the language spoken at the southeast end of Georgia Strait, Wayne Suttles found terms to describe each stage of its cycle: "flooding tide," "be flooding," "ebbing tide," "be ebbing," "high tide," "be just high water," "low tide," "be in a period of half-tides," "be slack water." The continuous variations plotted the day as efficiently as any clock: one glance at the level and direction of the current and you'd know exactly how soon to begin paddling home for lunch. Under clear skies, the states of the tide could be synchronized with the movements of heavenly bodies—as the Kwakiutl Indians showed Galiano and Valdés the time of slack water at Arran Rapids, by pointing at the mountaintop over which the sun should stand before the Dons attempted the passage.

The tide—calendar as well as clock—mapped the Indian year. In the Pacific Northwest, the two lowest tides of the year occur at local noon within a few days of the summer solstice, when the moon is full, and at midnight close to the winter solstice, when the moon is dark. Both events were celebrated. Families swarmed over the beaches to harvest shellfish during the midday summer lows. On the midnight winter lows, men and boys hunted wildfowl by torchlight. Suttles found Halkomelem words for the season: "shifts to daylight" meant the coming of spring, in March, when the big bull-tide lows, ideal for gathering clams, begin after sunrise; "shifts to dark" meant October, when the lowest lows occur before nightfall; "moon tide" described a low tide under a full moon, like the ones that signaled the summer clam-fest; "dark tide" referred to a low in the moon's final quarter, like the December wildfowling tides.

Afraid of meeting whirlpools in Whirlpool Rapids, I watched the tide as keenly as an Indian. The tables were not to be entirely trusted, especially at this time of year, when rising temperatures in the mountains filled the river with snowmelt: the torrent of freshwater, escaping to the sea, could easily overmaster a weak flood and throw a monkey-wrench into the works of the tidal clock. Strong offshore winds or abnormal atmospheric pressure were also likely to screw up the computer-modeled predictions. In the last 24 hours, a fifty-plus-knot wind had been blowing off Cape Scott, and the pressure was way down in the barograph's bass register.

The scrolled current-lines grew lazier and more indistinct as the flood dwindled to a trickle. Off Lyall Island, eight miles short of the rapids, I could sense the brimming stillness of high-water slack—where the sea seems to draw breath, the land to be afloat on a painted lake. The Halkomelem word for it was *xtlúnexam*. According to Thom Hess's *Dictionary of Puget Sound Salish*, when a story began with an image of water in this moment of stasis—mirror-like, without a ripple—a happy ending was guaranteed. Of these upbeat calm-water stories, though, I hadn't yet managed to find one.

Within five minutes, the sea was on the move again; thimble-sized vortices slid diagonally across the grain of the emerging current, and the Garmin showed the boat to be travel-ing steadily faster over the ground than through the water. Rid-ing the friendly tide, with the blood now back in my fingers, I could afford to take time out for a small diversion.

Where does the word "nookie" come from? "Prob. from *nook*," opines Wentworth and Flexner's *Dictionary of Ameri-can Slang*, in an untypically spiritless shot in the dark. Joseph Ingraham, cruising the Charlottes in 1791–92, compiled a rough-and-ready vocabulary of essential Haida words. The first and most important word on the list was for sea-otter pelt: "nuckky." In 1907, long after the sea otter had been hunted to near extinction, Franz Boas noted that the Bella Bella word for fur seal was "nukwe." By the early 1800s, several thousand American sailors—always generous contributors to vernacular English—were using "nookie" to mean something furry, soft, and precious. Captain Van would have gone from village to vil-lage, earnestly asking for nookie.

Far to the south, a tear in the sky exposed a ragged strip of blue behind the clouds; and a dog's-breath of air, from the southeast, not the forecast northwest, wrinkled the water. Whirlpool Rapids, now steaming into view, lay where the chan-nel was blocked on its western side by a bold wooded bluff with an offlying cigar-shaped island, which squeezed the tide into a firehose-jet.

The whirlpools formed at the downtide end of the pass, where the stream of fast water rubbed against the pools of slack on either side. A seven-knot current travels at nearly twelve feet per second—a fierce speed when applied to the rim of a baby vortex whose diameter is just an inch or two. This was like setting a gyroscope in motion with a long tug on a wound-up thread; the spinning vortex grew into a hungry, self-propelling eddy with a deepening center—a Kansas twister made of water.

As tornadoes do, whirlpools wander on wayward and arbitrary tracks that make them seem full of inscrutable purpose. A whirlpool might suddenly lunge sideways to snatch at a canoe, or veer off as abruptly as a shark declining to accept the bait. Indian literature dwelled on the skittish humor of whirlpools, their taste for human flesh, and their extreme sensitivity to fancied slights. In exchange for a safe passage, they required to be fed. The Tsimshian whirlpool of Getemnax, for instance, was partial to an offering of fat from the kidneys of a mountain goat. In one story, it was deeply offended by a group of young men who not only failed to provide the fat but also tried to smuggle past it an adolescent girl in the middle of her first menstrual period. They took the precaution of putting the girl and her grandmother in a separate canoe, and covering them with blankets, before towing them through the rapids; the whirlpool, undeceived, swallowed the men, breaking the towrope, and left the women safe but adrift.

In its emphasis on caution, respect, due preparation, and the consequences of bad timing, the story might have earned a place in Lecky's *Wrinkles in Practical Navigation*. I appeased the charted monsters by offering them hours of apprehension beforehand, by checking and rechecking the tide tables, and by allowing whirlpools to invade my dreams. Going into a tidal pass, I wasn't above crossing my fingers or touching the wood of the binnacle. On land, I was a hardline skeptic; afloat, something else. I never whistled on the boat. I noticed—with a faint tremor of anxiety—when a Friday was the 13th. On occasion I would've been reassured by the presence on board of the caul of a newborn or the feather of a wren killed on 1 January—a custom that led to the wren becoming an endangered species on the Isle of Man, so highly did Manx sailors prize their lucky feathers.

Racing into the jaws of Whirlpool Rapids, doing ten knots over the ground, I was 65 minutes into the ebb and just in time. A big bowl-shaped eddy had developed in the lee of the island, its swirling sides like tar in a mixer. But it paid no attention to the boat, and no sooner had I seen it than the tide sucked the boat past, out toward Johnstone Strait and open ocean.

"Everywhere," wrote Lévi-Strauss, meaning on the Northwest coast, "there emerges a parallelism between these natural disorders [like whirlpools associated with named monsters] and those which attack familial and social life." But of course! The safe management of a canoe through tidal rapids and rough water was the first requirement for survival in these parts—an experience that supplied an inevitable metaphor for the conduct of life. Drowning in a whirlpool was probably the culture's single most vivid image of catastrophe: the sudden loss of control, the upset boat, the bodies in the water, the overpowering current, the sucking down into the abyss. If you tried to imagine the consequences of, say, killing your brother, or sleeping with your sister, they would naturally present themselves in terms of the whirlpool, the earthquake, the *tsunami*—just as the canoe was seen as the vessel of life, from the canoe-cradles in which babies were rocked to those used for air burials in the trees. Bad social behavior was like careless canoeing, and got you into much the same kind of deep water. Here, where life was seen as a voyage through a multitude of natural hazards, it was hardly surprising that Lévi-Strauss should discover that the Indians' sea stories were really lightly coded encryptions of basic social rules, like the prohibitions against incest, murder, laziness, and egotism.

Maybe they order these things differently in French, but in English the fun of maritime metaphor goes very nearly as deep as it did in the Kwakiutl and Haida languages. We see things out to the bitter end (anchored in a storm, you let out all the cable you can to save the ship, and at last you reach the bitter end, the remaining length of chain in the locker, nearest to the bitts, around which it is secured; the ship eventually goes down, of course.) When surprised, you are taken aback, caught head-to-wind; when things go easily for you, it's plain (correctly, *plane*) sailing. Your manner is aloof (or *a-luff*); you let things go by the board; you need a loan to tide you over; coming home from the pub, three sheets to the wind, you lose your bearings . . . Both Robert Louis Stevenson, a Scot, and Elias Canetti, from Bulgaria and Vienna, observed that the Englishman has a deep-rooted habit of thinking of himself as the captain of a ship at sea; as Stevenson wrote, "a man from Bedfordshire, who does not know one end of the ship from the other until she begins to move, swaggers [on a Channel packet] with a sense of hereditary nautical experience." Taken by and large (as one assesses a ship in terms of her capacity to sail close to the wind, or "by," and off the wind, with sheets eased, or "large"), the English are in a good position to understand why Northwest Indians were inclined to see the whole of human life as something you do in a canoe.

IN OPEN water now, I killed the engine, unfurled the genoa, and let the boat coast quietly on the breeze while I tried to raise a marine operator on the VHF. Clicking through radio channels containing only static, I at last found a voice from the station at Alert Bay, the Kwakiutl reserve on Cormorant Island, and put through a call to Seattle.

Radio amplified the ringing tone, whose forlorn throbbing filled the boat. There's an audible difference between the sound of a telephone that will, in a few moments, be answered, and one that, at best, will say: "This is Jean . . . please leave a message."

The words had the volume and sound quality of an announcement echoing through the porcelain tunnels of the London tube. "Mind the gap, please. Mind the gap!"

In a calm sea, the first sign of turbulent water ahead is often a slight roughening of the horizon line, like the deckle edge along the top of an invitation card. *Odd,* you think, but pay it no special attention. Only later do you realize it was a signal to batten down the hatches.

THE GREAT outpouring of tide from the interior had smoothed the walls of Johnstone Strait, a gully forty miles long and a thousand feet deep, between Vancouver Island and the labyrinth of smaller islands to the north. The place had an unpleasant reputation as a wind funnel, but that morning the southeasterly was blowing at a gentle ten to twelve knots, just enough to keep the boat moving nicely under sail. With the sun now breaking through the clouds and silvering the water, the strait was a cheering sight after my string of lonely days: a broad marine highway on which orderly lines of coasters, fishing boats, tugs, and barges were following the posted route between Puget Sound and Alaska. The skipper of a Seattle-registered purse-seiner stepped out from his freshly painted wheelhouse to give me a wave as he swept past; we were both of us now far enough away from our shared home port for the usual tribal hostilities between yachts and working boats to be forgotten.

The narrow entrance to Port Neville opened and closed again in what seemed like a flash, with the boat traveling much faster than the tide tables said it should. I was sailing at five knots, but the land was going past at eight, or so the GPS consistently reported. My best guess was that I was enjoying the benefit of "slippery water."

Seawater, laden with chlorides and minerals, is heavier than fresh. When a river meets the sea, it's liable to spill out in a wide fan across the top of the denser, saline water. So the brackish surface layer of an estuary can move independently of the saltwater tide below, sliding over it in a continuous ebb current, even when the deep tide is on the flood. Something like this was happening now on Johnstone Strait. The boat was riding on the fast surface current, while the true tide rolled sluggishly westward at a knot or less. I dipped a bucket over the side, and tried the water on my tongue: powerfully salty, not brackish at all. But I clung to the slippery-water theory, a useful explanation of all sorts of inconsistencies between the tables and the erratic behavior of the actual tide.

I'd just stowed my bucket when a sudden rush of wind came down the funnel of the strait, like an unprovoked punch delivered out of nowhere. The boat corkscrewed. The genoa-sheet, bar-tight, groaned on the drum of the winch. I feared for the stitching of the sail as the fabric swelled under the impact of the wind, which had begun to yodel nastily in the rigging. In no time at all, the ruffled water changed to a short, steep, breaking sea.

Sunlit waves never frighten anyone half so much as the same waves under a sullen sky. These waves were full of light and life. The sun, shining clean through their tops, rendered them an opalescent milky green, which darkened, as the wave thickened around the middle, to the turquoise of a peacock's tail. Algae and phytoplankton gave them the color of a coastal sea dense with vegetable matter, like frigid minestrone.

I had meant to go on to Alert Bay, to meet the Kwakiutl, but the wind nixed that plan. Thirty knots was more than I could safely handle. As the fetch of the strait lengthened, the waves climbed and the boat seesawed over them, crashing into each trough and trying to bury its nose in the wave immediately

ahead. Drenched in spray, and by the occasional bucketful of
solid green water, I hung onto the wheel, spinning it violently
to keep it to a more-or-less steady downwind course. I had too
much sail up, but it was too late now to mess around with flail-
ing sheets and furling-line. For more than an hour the boat ran
away with me, rearing and plunging as if bent on trying to cata-
pult its rider into the sparkling soup.

Even in high sunshine, I had no appetite for this. I had
learned to sail too late in life to acquire a real seaman's instinct
for what to do when the wind gets up and the sea growls. I had to
listen to the creaking machinery of my own reason as I thought,
not felt, my way through the rising waves, trying to figure out
what on earth I'd do when the mast snapped off at the root, as
it surely would, and soon. I remembered some book or other
saying that heavy-duty wire cutters were essential onboard. I
had none. So the 46-foot mast, now in the water, trapped by a
cat's-cradle of steel rigging, would work on the hull as a battering ram, until it punched a hole amidships and the boat went
down in a string of big bubbles. Wrenching the wheel to starboard, hoping to correct the boat's sideways slew down a wave,
I could already hear the crunch of the severed mast breaking
through into the gallery, smashing plates and glasses, letting
the sea rush in. I was always the coward, who dies many times
before his death.

Nine miles on from Port Neville was a merciful gap in the
north wall of the strait, where the Broken Islands were strewn
across the entrance to Havannah Channel. I ran for cover there,

with the boat skidding into the lee on a crackling surge of foam. The mast still stood. The sun shone. A seal, basking on a rock, opened an eye at my arrival and slid soundlessly into the calm water, making not a ripple.

ON DECK

SYLVIA PLATH

One of the 20th century's major poets, Sylvia Plath (1932–1963) was born in Massachusetts; her father, a professor of German and zoology at Boston University, died when Plath was eight. Though she had unsuccessfully attempted suicide while a student at Smith College, she graduated in 1955 and won a Fulbright scholarship to Cambridge, England. There she met the British poet Ted Hughes; they married in 1956. Her first book of poems, *The Colossus,* was published in 1960, and a novel, *The Bell Jar,* appeared in 1963. By then she and Hughes had separated; she committed suicide in London the same year. After Plath's death, Hughes oversaw the publication of several works of her prose, children's literature, her journals, and further collections of poetry, including *Ariel* (1965) and the relatively calm series of poems, *Crossing the Water* (1971), the source of this laconic assessment of her fellow passengers on a cross-Atlantic voyage.

. . .

Midnight in the mid-Atlantic. On deck.
Wrapped up in themselves as in thick veiling
And mute as mannequins in a dress shop,
Some few passengers keep track
Of the old star-map on the ceiling.
Tiny and far, a single ship

Lit like a two-tired wedding cake
Carries its candles slowly off.
Now there is nothing much to look at.
Still nobody will move or speak—
The bingo players, the players at love
On a square no bigger than a carpet

Are hustled over the crests and troughs,
Each stalled in his particular minute
And castled in it like a king.
Small drops spot their coats, their gloves:
They fly too fast to feel the wet.
Anything can happen where they are going.

The untidy lady revivalist
For whom the good Lord provides (He gave
Her a pocketbook, a pearl hatpin
And seven winter coats last August)
Prays under her breath that she may save
The art students in West Berlin.

The astrologer at her elbow (a Leo)
Picked his trip-date by the stars.
He is gratified by the absence of icecakes.
He'll be rich in a year (and he should know)
Selling the Welsh and English mothers
Nativities at two-and-six.

And the white-haired jeweller from
    Denmark is carving
A perfectly faceted wife to wait
On him hand and foot, quiet as a diamond.
Moony balloons tied by a string
To their owners' wrists, the light dreams float
To be let loose at news of land.

THE SEA TOOK ITS CUE

YANN MARTEL

Born in Spain in 1963, the son of Quebec poet and diplomat Émile Martel, Yann Martel has lived a peripatetic life, growing up in Alaska, Canada, Costa Rica, France, and Mexico, and living as an adult in Iran, Turkey, India, and Germany. He graduated from Trent University, Peterborough, with a degree in philosophy, and has taught a course at the University of Berlin called "Meeting the Other: The Animal in Western Literature." His first book, a collection of stories titled *The Facts Behind the Helsinki Roccamatios*, appeared in 1993 and was followed by a novel, *Self*, in 1996. But his second novel, *The Life of Pi* (2001), excerpted here, has garnered the most attention, winning the Hugh MacLennan Prize as well as the prestigious Man Booker Prize in 2002. It concerns a man and a tiger trapped aboard a drifting lifeboat on the Pacific Ocean, and it challenges the romantic aspects of the relationship between man and nature. Martel now lives in Saskatoon, Saskatchewan.

THE STORM CAME on slowly one afternoon. The clouds looked as if they were stumbling along before the wind, frightened. The sea took its cue. It started rising and falling in a manner that made my heart sink. I took in the solar stills and the net. Oh, you should have seen that landscape! What I had seen up till now were mere hillocks of water. These swells were truly mountains. The valleys we found ourselves in were so deep they were gloomy. Their sides were so steep the lifeboat started sliding down them, nearly surfing. The raft was getting exceptionally rough treatment, being pulled out of the water and dragged along bouncing every which way. I deployed both sea anchors fully, at different lengths so that they would not interfere with each other.

Climbing the giant swells, the boat clung to the sea anchors like a mountain climber to a rope. We would rush up until we reached a snow-white crest in a burst of light and foam and a tipping forward of the lifeboat. The view would be clear for miles around. But the mountain would shift, and the ground beneath us would start sinking in a most stomach-sickening way. In no time we would be sitting once again at the bottom of a dark valley, different from the last but the same, with thousands of tons of water hovering above us and with only our flimsy lightness to save us. The land would move once more, the sea-anchor ropes would snap to tautness, and the roller coaster would start again.

The sea anchors did their job well—in fact, nearly too well. Every swell at its crest wanted to take us for a tumble, but the anchors, beyond the crest, heaved mightily and pulled us through, but at the expense of pulling the front of the boat down. The result was an explosion of foam and spray at the bow. I was soaked through and through each time.

Then a swell came up that was particularly intent on taking us along. This time the bow vanished underwater. I was shocked and chilled and scared witless. I barely managed to hold on. The boat was swamped. I heard Richard Parker roar. I felt death was upon us. The only choice left to me was death by water or death by animal. I chose death by animal.

When we sank down the back of the swell, I jumped onto the tarpaulin and unrolled it towards the stern, closing in Richard Parker. If he protested, I did not hear him. Faster than a sewing machine working a piece of cloth, I hooked down the tarpaulin on both sides of the boat. We were climbing again. The boat was lurching upwards steadily. It was hard to keep my balance. The lifeboat was now covered and the tarpaulin battened down, except at my end. I squeezed in between the side bench and the tarpaulin and pulled the remaining tarpaulin over my head. I did not have much space. Between bench and gunnel there was twelve inches, and the side benches were only one and a half feet wide. But I was not so foolhardy, even in the face of death, as to move onto the floor of the boat. There were four hooks left to catch. I slipped a hand through the opening and worked the rope. With each hook done, it was getting harder to get the next. I managed two. Two hooks left. The boat was rushing upwards in a smooth and unceasing motion.

The incline was over thirty degrees. I could feel myself being pulled down towards the stern. Twisting my hand frantically I succeeded in catching one more hook with the rope. It was the best I could do. This was not a job meant to be done from the inside of the lifeboat but from the outside. I pulled hard on the rope, something made easier by the fact that holding on to it was preventing me from sliding down the length of the boat. The boat swiftly passed a forty-five-degree incline.

We must have been at a sixty-degree incline when we reached the summit of the swell and broke through its crest onto the other side. The smallest portion of the swell's supply of water crashed down on us. I felt as if I were being pummelled by a great fist. The lifeboat abruptly tilted forward and everything was reversed: I was now at the lower end of the lifeboat, and the water that had swamped it, with a tiger soaking in it, came my way. I did not feel the tiger—I had no precise idea of where Richard Parker was; it was pitch-black beneath the tarpaulin—but before we reached the next valley I was half-drowned.

For the rest of that day and into the night, we went up and down, up and down, up and down, until terror became monotonous and was replace by numbness and a complete giving-up. I held on to the tarpaulin rope with one hand and the edge of the bow bench with the other, while my body lay flat against the side bench. In this position—water pouring in, water pouring out—the tarpaulin beat me to a pulp, I was soaked and chilled, and I was bruised and cut by bones and turtle shells. The noise of the storm was constant, as was Richard Parker's snarling.

Sometime during the night my mind noted that the storm was over. We were bobbing on the sea in a normal manner. Through a tear in the tarpaulin I glimpsed the night sky. Starry and cloudless. I undid the tarpaulin and lay on top of it.

I noticed the loss of the raft at dawn. All that was left of it were two tied oars and the life jacket between them. They had the same effect on me as the last standing beam of a burnt-down house would have on a householder. I turned and scrutinized every quarter of the horizon. Nothing. My little marine town had vanished. That the sea anchors, miraculously, were not lost—they continued to tug at the lifeboat faithfully—was a consolation that had no effect. The loss of the raft was perhaps not fatal to my body, but it felt fatal to my spirits.

The boat was in a sorry state. The tarpaulin was torn in several places, some tears evidently the work of Richard Parker's claws. Much of our food was gone, either lost overboard or destroyed by the water that had come in. I was sore all over and had a bad cut on my thigh; the wound was swollen and white. I was nearly too afraid to check the contents of the locker. Thank God none of the water bags had split. The net and the solar stills, which I had not entirely deflated, had filled the empty space and prevented the bags from moving too much.

I felt exhausted and depressed. I unhooked the tarpaulin at the stern. Richard Parker was so silent I wondered whether he had drowned. He hadn't. As I rolled back the tarpaulin to the middle bench and daylight came to him, he stirred and growled. He climbed out of the water and set himself on the stern bench.

I took out needle and thread and went about mending the tears in the tarpaulin.

Later I tied one of the buckets to a rope and bailed out the boat. Richard Parker watched me distractedly. He seemed to find nearly everything I did boring. The day was hot and I proceeded slowly. One haul brought me something I had lost. I considered it. Cradled in the palm of my hand was all that remained between me and death: the last of the orange whistles.

I WAS on the tarpaulin, wrapped in a blanket, sleeping and dreaming and awakening and daydreaming and generally passing the time. There was a steady breeze. From time to time spray was blown off the crest of a wave and wet the boat. Richard Parker had disappeared under the tarpaulin. He liked neither getting wet nor the ups and downs of the boat. But the sky was blue, the air was warm, and the sea was regular in its motion. I awoke because there was a blast. I opened my eyes and saw water in the sky. It crashed down on me. I looked up again. Cloudless blue sky. There was another blast, to my left, not as powerful as the first. Richard Parker growled fiercely. More water crashed against me. It had an unpleasant smell.

I looked over the edge of the boat. The first thing I saw was a large black object floating in the water. It took me a few seconds to understand what it was. An arching wrinkle around its edge was my clue. It was an eye. It was a whale. Its eye, the size of my head, was looking directly at me.

Richard Parker came up from beneath the tarpaulin. He hissed. I sensed from a slight change in the glint of the whale's eye that it was now looking at Richard Parker. It gazed for thirty seconds or so before gently sinking under. I worried that it might strike us with its tail, but it went straight down and vanished in the dark blue. Its tail was a huge, fading, round bracket.

I believe it was a whale looking for a mate. It must have decided that my size wouldn't do, and besides, I already seemed to have a mate.

We saw a number of whales but none so close up as that first one. I would be alerted to their presence by their spouting. They would emerge a short distance away, sometimes three or four of them, a short-lived archipelago of volcanic islands. These gentle behemoths always lifted my spirits. I was convinced that they understood my condition, that at the sight of me one of them exclaimed, "Oh! It's that castaway with the pussy cat Bamphoo was telling me about. Poor boy. Hope he has enough plankton. I must tell Mumphoo and Tomphoo and Stimphoo about him. I wonder if there isn't a ship around I could alert. His mother would be very happy to see him. Goodbye, my boy. I'll try to help. My name's Pimphoo." And so, through the grapevine, every whale in the Pacific knew of me, and I would have been saved long ago if Pimphoo hadn't sought help from a Japanese ship whose dastardly crew harpooned her, the same fate as befell Lamphoo at the hands of a Norwegian ship. The hunting of whales is a heinous crime.

Dolphins were a fairly regular vision. One group stayed with us a whole day and night. They were very gay. Their plunging and turning and racing just beneath the hull seemed to have no purpose other than sporting fun. I tried to catch one. But none came close to the gaff. And even if they had, they were too fast and too big. I gave up and just watched them.

I saw six birds in all. I took each one to be an angel announcing nearby land. But these were seafaring birds that could span the Pacific with hardly a flutter of the wings. I watched them with awe and envy and self-pity.

Twice I saw an albatross. Each flew by high in the air without taking any notice of us. I stared with my mouth open. They were something supernatural and incomprehensible.

Another time, a short distance from the boat, two Wilson's petrels skimmed by, feet skipping on the water. They, too, took no notice of us, and left me similarly amazed.

We at last attracted the attention of a short-tailed shearwater. It circled above us, eventually dropping down. It kicked out its legs, turned its wings, and alighted in the water, floating as lightly as a cork. It eyed me with curiosity. I quickly baited a hook with a bit of flying fish and threw the line its way. I put no weights on the line and had difficulty getting it close to the bird. On my third try the bird paddled up to the sinking bait and plunged its head underwater to get at it. My heart pounded with excitement. I did not pull on the line for some seconds. When I did, the bird merely squawked and regurgitated what it had just swallowed. Before I could try again, it unfolded its wings and pulled itself up into the air. Within two, three beatings of its wings it was on its way.

I had better luck with a masked booby. It appeared out of nowhere, gliding towards us, wings spanning over three feet. It landed on the gunnel within hand's reach of me. Its round eyes took me in, the expression puzzled and serious. It was a large bird with a pure snowy white body and wings that were jet-black at their tips and rear edges. Its big, bulbous head had a very pointed orange-yellow beak and the red eyes behind the black mask made it look like a thief who had had a very long night. Only the oversized, brown webbed feet left something to be desired in their design. The bird was fearless. It spent several minutes tweaking its feathers with its beak, exposing soft down. When it was finished, it looked up and everything fell into place, and it showed itself for what it was: a smooth, beautiful aerodynamic airship. When I offered it a bit of dorado, it pecked it out of my hand, jabbing the palm.

I broke its neck by leveraging its head backwards, one hand pushing up the beak, the other holding the neck. The feathers were so well attached that when I started pulling them out, skin came off—I was not plucking the bird; I was tearing it apart. It was light enough as it was, a volume with no weight. I took the knife and skinned it instead. For its size there was a disappointing amount of flesh, only a little on its chest. It had a more chewy texture than dorado flesh, but I didn't find there was much of a difference in taste. In its stomach, besides the morsel of dorado I had just given it, I found three small fish. After rinsing them of digestive juices, I ate them. I ate the bird's heart, liver and lungs. I swallowed its eyes and tongue with a gulp of water. I crushed its head and picked out its small brain. I ate the webbings of its feet. The rest of the bird was skin, bone and feathers. I dropped it beyond the edge of the tarpaulin for Richard Parker, who hadn't seen the bird arrive. An orange paw reached out.

Days later feathers and down were still floating up from his den and being blown out to sea. Those that landed in the water were swallowed by fish.

None of the birds ever announced land.

ONCE THERE was lightning. The sky was so black, day looked like night. The downpour was heavy. I heard thunder far away. I thought it would stay at that. But a wind came up, throwing the rain this way and that. Right after, a white splinter came crashing down from the sky, puncturing the water. It was some distance from the lifeboat, but the effect was perfectly visible. The water was shot through with what looked like white roots; briefly, a great celestial tree stood in the ocean. I had never imagined such a thing possible, lightning striking the sea. The clap of thunder was tremendous. The flash of light was incredibly vivid.

I turned to Richard Parker and said, "Look, Richard Parker, a bolt of lightning." I saw how he felt about it. He was flat on the floor of the boat, limbs splayed and visibly trembling.

The effect on me was completely the opposite. It was something to pull me out of my limited mortal ways and thrust me into a state of exalted wonder.

Suddenly a bolt struck much closer. Perhaps it was meant for us: we had just fallen off the crest of a swell and were sinking down its back when its top was hit. There was an explosion of hot air and hot water. For two, perhaps three seconds, a gigantic, blinding white shard of glass from a broken cosmic window danced in the sky, insubstantial yet overwhelmingly powerful. Ten thousand trumpets and twenty thousand drums could not have made as much noise as that bolt of lightning; it was positively deafening. The sea turned white and all colour disappeared. Everything was either pure white light or pure black shadow. The light did not seem to illuminate so much as to penetrate. As quickly as it appeared, the bolt vanished—the spray of hot water had not finished landing upon us and already it was gone. The punished swell returned to black and rolled on indifferently.

I was dazed, thunderstruck—nearly in the true sense of the word. But not afraid.

"Praise be to Allah, Lord of All Worlds, the Compassionate, the Merciful, Ruler of Judgment Day!" I muttered. To Richard Parker I shouted, "Stop your trembling! This is miracle. This is an outbreak of divinity. This is . . . this is . . ." I could not find what it was, this thing so vast and fantastic. I was breathless and wordless. I lay back on the tarpaulin, arms and legs spread wide. The rain chilled me to the bone. But I was smiling. I remember that close encounter with electrocution and third-degree burns as one of the few times during my ordeal when I felt genuine happiness.

At moments of wonder it is easy to avoid small thinking, to entertain thoughts that span the universe, that capture both thunder and tinkle, thick and thin, the near and the far.

SEA BURIAL

JAMES HAMILTON-PATERSON

Poet and novelist James Hamilton-Paterson was born in 1941 in London, where he worked as a teacher, reporter, and hospital porter before leaving England in 1979 to divide his time between Tuscany and the Phillipines. Something of a recluse, he describes himself as "a rat-poor literary drifter." His first novel, *Gerontius* (1989), won the Whitbread Prize, and he has since published four others—praised by Michael Ondaatje for their "wonderful mongrel quality"—as well as two volumes of poetry and five works of nonfiction, including *Three Miles Down* (1998), his account of joining a search for gold bullion sunk during the Second World War. In this nonfiction story he describes the effect on a Filipino fishing-boat crew of coming upon a drifting boat containing a corpse.

. . .

Do you remember this?

A broken engine; the hours' becalming; an empty ocean still as a lake of mercury. It was soundless to the horizon and our small noises placed us at the centre of the universe, unique in our activity. From time to time a spanner clinked, a bare foot bumped a thwart. From the vinyl-scented shade of a rigged tarpaulin we watched our tiny ripples become visible only as they left the *Medevina*'s shadow, trembling outward, as if the shadow's edge were the actual hull, our whole craft insubstantial, no more than an airy nothing which had briefly come between sun and sea. The mutter of voices *(Try this. It's rusty. The gasket's ruined.)*, the rasp and flare of a match, the incense of a cigarette. The small splash of a handful of waste. And then, emerging from the shadow into gorgeous colour like the tip of a kingfisher's wing, an iridescent oil-stain flashing its molecules, splitting the spectrum and creeping out across the water. Do you remember how dazzling it was? That spreading puddle of hues in a still world of primary blue? Greens and purple, golds and pinks, rubies and violets, forming and re-forming, pooling and glittering minutely so the fascinated mind drew ever closer to its surface and fell into a microscope's gaze such that the twinkle and sputter of evaporation almost became visible, the spirituous fractions boiling off in order of their volatility.

The sun climbed and remained stuck at the top of the sky. Sometimes we stood up or wandered aft to peer at the dismantled carburettor. The parts were black with oil and rust—deformed, even: corroded artefacts turned up by a plough rather than precision-engineered components. Our shifting weight as we moved about the narrow boat made one bamboo outrigger gently dent the water, the other rise and shed a line of droplets.

The brilliant oil-stain fractured. Feathers and petals broke off, some drifting perversely back into our shadow and winking out. A flotilla of melding islets moved into the glare beyond the outrigger, sending back scorching chromatic flashes. The hours passed. Fish and rice to eat, the bowls washed over the side and fat replenishing the film until—do you remember?—a peacock sheen surrounded our soundless universe, marbled and swirled and striated. In a halo of specious glory our little boat sat and baked, breathing out its rainbowed anima.

No, you will not have forgotten; not in the light of what was to happen later, not in the particular isolating light in which individual events were picked out with such intensity.

Now and then a fish rose, but languidly, as if its head had difficulty breaking the surface tension, so thick was the water's skin. Several pairs of eyes would remain on the resealed hole where snout or fin had protruded for an instant. At length a flying fish broke completely out, tail whirring the water's surface like the propellor of a planing speedboat and leaving a straight scar of irregular dashes for sixty yards before vanishing into an invisible notch. This was a fishing boat, after all, and at last someone aroused himself out of his lethargy enough to bait a hook and drop it into the rectangle of water enclosed by an outrigger. It was as much for something to do as a gesture of habit.

It was mid-afternoon before the engine started. Our companions murmured their relief. We had lost six hours. The blocks of ice in the insulated chests would be that much smaller. Nobody had opened the lids to look, for fear of accelerating the process. Now we could spend fewer than four hours at the lobster beds, even if the motor kept going and took us there before midnight. You will not have forgotten how precarious these trips were, ninety miles each way. If all went well we could fill half the chests with lobsters, having transferred the remaining ice to the other half to pack around fish. Any serious delay on the way back might mean the fish were lost. And this quite apart from the usual risks of dodging coastguard cutters alert for illegal fishermen. Edgy times; but grounded in comradeship and marked, as always, by heightened senses.

How vivid, still, are the seagoing smells? Oily bilges, fish entrails, a freshly lit cigarette drawn through salt pepper? And at night, if you were not diving, the compressor's exhaust fumes, its lethal monoxides, barking and blattering our darkened boat's position for anyone to hear. But a shift of wind might gently lay its hand on a cheek and turn your head like a weathervane, pointing your nostrils into the smell of unseen land: forest and rot and copra, jasmine, mimosa and ylang-ylang. And you may have thought of the strangeness of it, sitting there in night's scented cocoon, propped up by nails and timber in the middle of the water while men you knew like brothers worked away in the fish mines far beneath the boat, their dim torchlight, opening up fugitive seams and corridors. Their wooden goggles and floating hair.

And behind everything, the economics: the tanks of fuel we carried set against the miles we needed to cover; the ice matched with that and the anticipated size of the catch; the future price of fish in the market half a week away; profits eaten up by repairs. The fisherman's immemorial equations, whose hidden term is time. Tides and currents, nightfall and winds, the rising of the moon: all determine whether he is too early, too late, or punctual for the flow of fish he is banking on at his journey's end.

So we were already late; but the captain said Push on. Push on, go (pointing with jutting lips to the speckless ocean's rim). To turn and head for home was too safe, too undisguised a loss of fuel and effort. Follow the sun, now curving a south-westering course. In this way we reached the moment when our prow was aimed directly at where, in one corner of the day-long featureless sky, evening clouds were beginning to form a range of wool mountains above an invisible coast. It was still too early for pinkish colours. The peaks were white and blue-and-white, undershadowed with pearl: glittering snowfields which convection was thrusting into pinnacles and spires even as we watched, transforming the alps into the skyline of an impossible town. There, among amorphous towers and eroding castles, an insane architect was busy opening up sly passages, glimpses of alleys, vistas of tall windows and bent porticoes whose very act of moulding held out the constant promise of disclosure. Glancing away for a moment and then looking back, the eye would catch these apertures at the tantalizing instant of being sealed by vapour, blocked by soundless landslides, erased for ever. Even as the gaze scrambled back down crumbling stairways leading nowhere, the great gates were slamming all around in silence. And always, as they closed or melted, they left behind

the faintest air of having successfully denied, or having withheld a view of some innermost chamber or secret courtyard now
buried deep within palisades.

Meanwhile, the mercury ocean across which we had been
heading was gone. In its place a glassy violaceous swell reflected
this soft metropolis so that one image leaned above the other,
the lower scarcely distorted. And it was on this, dead ahead,
you will remember we first saw the tiny black insect of another
boat. The only visible object on the ocean's face, it lay in our
path with the punctuality of an omen. Without needing to alter
course by a degree we gradually overhauled the lone fisherman
as he sat in the celestial city's mirrored thoroughfares.

The captain eased the nylon string which held the throttle so
the engine note fell to a mutter and the *Medevina* lost way. With
the rudder slightly over we began a gentle curve which took us
within hailing distance of the fisherman, but not so close that our
wake would swamp him. As to what we already thought, can
you remember that? Even though we had passed many identi-
cal craft on previous expeditions, can you remember if you had
taken in the absence of a mast and rice-sack sail, or the fact that
the boat's smallness and the man's position in it made it obvious
there could be no engine? Even as we came abreast thirty yards
off, had you appreciated that nobody under paddle-power alone
would allow himself to drift so far out to sea that no land was
visible at any point of the compass? A stocky man, the boat's
occupant was wedged comfortably low on the bottom boards,
watching our approach from beneath the brim of a hat shaped

like a straw lampshade. A fishing line was stretched the free-board's short distance between one hand and the water.

"Oy, *paré!*" called our captain, allowing us to laze across his bows, then around to the other side. The fisherman's face did not turn, however, and something about his posture had forestalled any jocular shouts of "*Hoy gising!* Wake up there!" The captain only said for all of us, softly, "*Yari na. Patay na.*" And so we completed our circle, staring at the dead man, the water at our stern dimpling and crawling above the scarcely revolving screw. There was still no breath of wind; but possibly even at a saunter our own larger vessel with its spread awning leaned against enough air lazily to displace it, for by the time we had gone entirely around the fisherman a waft of corruption had reached us. There, in the early evening light amid the shattered debris of clouds, he sat and exhaled the gases of his own corporeal breakdown.

ACKNOWLEDGMENTS

"Noah Would Not Give Up Even a Splinter" excerpted from *In Fond Remembrance of Me* by Howard Norman (New York: Farrar, Straus and Giroux, 2005).

"The Sleep at Sea" excerpted from Homer's *The Odyssey*, translated by Stephen Heighton in *The Address Book*. Reprinted with permission from House of Anansi Press.

"The Seafarer" excerpted from "The Seafarer," translated by Ezra Pound in *Ripostes* (London: Stephen Swift and Company, 1912).

"A Scene of Horrible Calamities" excerpted from *Narrative of the Shipwreck and Sufferings of Miss Ann Saunders* by Ann Saunders (Providence: Z.S. Crossmon, 1827).

"Phosphorescence of the Sea" excerpted from *Journal of Researches* by Charles Darwin (London: Henry Colburn, 1839).

"The Pacific" excerpted from *Moby-Dick* by Herman Melville (New York, 1851).

Fowles. Reprinted by permission of Henry Holt and Company, LLC and with permission from Jonathan Cape.

"The Sea Is History" reproduced from *Collected Poems 1948–1984* by Derek Walcott (New York: Farrar, Straus and Giroux, 1986).

"The Boat Journey" excerpted from *The Voyage of the Narwhal* by Andrea Barrett. Copyright © 1998 by Andrea Barrett. Used by permission of W.W. Norton & Company, Inc

"Sky Like a Grubby Washcloth" excerpted from *Passage to Juneau* by Jonathan Raban. Copyright © 1999 by Jonathan Raban. Used by permission of Pantheon Books, a division of Random House, Inc.

"On Deck" excerpted from *Crossing the Water* by Sylvia Plath. Copyright © The estate of Sylvia Plath. Used by permission of Faber and Faber Ltd. Copyright © 1971 by Ted Hughes. Reprinted by permission of Harper Collins Publishers.

"The Sea Took Its Cue" excerpted from *Life of Pi* by Yann Martel. Copyright © Yann Martel. Reprinted by permission of Knopf Canada.

"Sea Burial" excerpted from *"Sea Burial"* by James Hamilton-Paterson. (New York: Granta U.S., 1998).

The David Suzuki Foundation works through science and education to protect the diversity of nature and our quality of life, now and for the future.

With a goal of achieving sustainability within a generation, the Foundation collaborates with scientists, business and industry, academia, government and non-governmental organizations. We seek the best research to provide innovative solutions that will help build a clean, competitive economy that does not threaten the natural services that support all life.

The Foundation is a federally registered independent charity, which is supported with the help of over 50,000 individual donors across Canada and around the world.

We invite you to become a member. For more information on how you can support our work, please contact us:

The David Suzuki Foundation
219–2211 West 4th Avenue
Vancouver, BC
Canada v6k 4s2
www.davidsuzuki.org
contact@davidsuzuki.org
Tel: 604-732-4228 · Fax: 604-732-0752

Checks can be made payable to The David Suzuki Foundation.
All donations are tax-deductible.
Canadian charitable registration: (BN) 12775 6716 RR0001
U.S. charitable registration: #94-3204049